MW00963046

Take a romantic cruise on the yacht *Kristiana* in pursuit of marital bliss...

Pat Rushford invites you to explore "the small, scattered islands of fanciful thinking" in *Love Is a Many Splintered Thing*. Join her and the *Kristiana's* owner and tour guide, Kansas Smith, for an imaginary voyage into the minds of men and women to discover what we *really* want from and for each other. Share the experiences of star-crossed lovers Samantha Jones and David Hartley — "a fictional but all-too-real couple" — as they progress from infatuation to fulfilling, realistic love. Together you'll explore:

- *The Fantasy Islands* Daydream of the ideal mate in the land of Man's Imagination and Eve's Estuary.
- *Expectation Caves* Face and conquer your greatest enemies — the seven dragons of false expectations.
- *Reality Straits* Wake up to the ultimate truths by entering the Temple of Doomed Relationships and the unseen world of causes of failed marriages.
- *Reconciliation Bay* Find hope, healing, and your inner spiritual self in God's peaceful Sanctuary and holy Presence.

So climb aboard the *Kristiana*. You will never forget the adventures, discoveries, and treasures of insight that await you.

LOVE
Is a Many
SPLINTERED
Thing

Also by Patricia H. Rushford

What Kids Need Most in a Mom
The Help, Hope, & Cope Book for People
With Aging Parents
Have You Hugged Your Teenager Today?
Caring for Your Sick Child
Kristen's Choice

By Jean Lush With Patricia H. Rushford

Emotional Phases of a Woman's Life

LOVE
Is a Many
SPLINTERED
Thing

Patricia H. Rushford

Fleming H. Revell Company
Old Tappan, New Jersey

Unless otherwise identified, Scripture quotations are from New American Standard Bible, © The Lockman Foundation 1960, 1962, 1963, 1968, 1971, 1972, 1973, 1975, 1977.

Scripture quotations marked NIV are from the Holy Bible, New International Version. Copyright © 1973, 1978, 1984 International Bible Society. Used by permission of Zondervan Bible Publishers.

Scripture quotations identified PHILLIPS are from THE NEW TESTAMENT IN MODERN ENGLISH, Revised Edition—J.B. Phillips, translator. © J.B. Phillips 1958, 1960, 1972. Used by permission of Macmillan Publishing Co., Inc.

Scripture quotations identified RSV are from the Revised Standard Version of the Bible, Copyrighted © 1946, 1952, 1971, by The Division of Christian Education of the National Council of the Churches of Christ in the United States of America, and are used by permission. All rights reserved.

Verses marked TLB are taken from *The Living Bible*, Copyright © 1971 by Tyndale House Publishers, Wheaton, Ill. Used by permission.

Fictional characters in this book do not exist outside the imagination of the author and have no relation to anyone bearing the same name or names. They are not inspired by any individual known or unknown to the author, and all incidents are pure fiction. In nonfiction examples, names and circumstances have been changed, and stories are used with the permission of the persons involved.

Library of Congress Cataloging-in-Publication Data

Rushford, Patricia H.
    Love is a many splintered thing / Patricia H. Rushford.
        p.   cm.
    ISBN 0-8007-5343-7
    1. Marriage—United States.   2. Interpersonal relations.   3. Love.
I. Title.
HQ734.R799   1990   90-8017
306.81′0973—dc20   CIP

All rights reserved. No part of this publication may be reproduced, stored in a retrieval system, or transmitted in any form or by any means—electronic, mechanical, photocopy, recording, or any other—except for brief quotations in printed reviews, without the prior permission of the publisher.

Copyright © 1990 by Patricia H. Rushford
Published by the Fleming H. Revell Company
Old Tappan, New Jersey 07675
Printed in the United States of America

TO Ron,
whom I adore and whose priceless love
I will cherish forever

Contents

Acknowledgments

My special thanks to:

My husband, Ron; Margo Power; William Vermillion; Gail Vonada; and Ann Reigelhuth for their sage advice and for taking time to proofread and critique my manuscript.

Anne Christian Buchanan for her wonderful editing skills, help, and encouragement.

All the men and women who took the time to share what they need most in one another.

LOVE
Is a Many
SPLINTERED
Thing

Chapter 1
The Battle Rages On

How do you begin a book on men and women and their needs? I wondered as I faced the empty computer screen. I suppose the best way to begin would be to share a few gems from my own reasonably happy relationship . . .

The Happy Couple

The word *happy* had no sooner appeared on my computer screen when my concentration was broken by Ron's bellow from the main bathroom.

"Pat! Doggone it! How many times do I have to tell you to shut the faucet completely off when you take a bath?"

"Oh no, not now," I moaned. "He must be paying bills again." I really didn't want to hear about the water, the electricity, and all the other things this particular argument would entail. So I yelled back, "I'm sorry, honey, I forgot!"

But did my humble (well, somewhat humble) apology satisfy him? He yelled even louder. "You'd think after all these years

13

you'd know what bugs me and try not to do it. Are you deliberately trying to drive me nuts?"

What could I say? Details are not now nor have they ever been my strong suit. After living with me for twenty-five years, Ron should know that. The tone of his voice told me he was asking for a fight. Far be it from me to disappoint the man.

"Oh, right!" I yelled. "I'm deliberately not turning off the faucet to drive you crazy. What's the big deal, anyway? You'd think I did this sort of thing every day!"

"You do! And another thing . . ."

As you can guess, our little problem exploded into a nasty argument. When it was over, and we'd kissed—okay, we didn't exactly kiss, but we did agree not to kill each other—I stomped back into my office to write.

"Ha! This is a joke." I scowled at the flashing green cursor on my computer screen. *How do I tell men and women what they need in one another when I feel like flushing my most recent "how to make your hubby happy" book down the toilet?*

Do you know how devastating it is to lose your cool and appear so blatantly imperfect when you're supposed to be coming off as an expert? Here I am, author of eight books, a counselor, a graduate student, and a registered nurse—and I'm fighting with my husband over a drippy faucet. *You're also human,* I reminded myself. "That's true enough," I answered as I focused on the mocking green cursor and wrote, "What men and women need most in one another is . . . is . . ."

I clenched my fists and yanked at my hair. Oh, pooh! What I needed most at that moment was a big hug, and I knew just where to get it.

I inched my way down the hall and found Ron standing at the window in the living room. I came up behind him and wrapped my arms around his chest. "Honey . . ." I sighed as he turned in my arms and hugged me back.

"Does this mean my absentminded professor's decided to turn over a new leaf?"

I punched him teasingly in the stomach. "You know I can't make rash promises like that. Besides, I do try. It's just that I get to thinking and . . ."

"You know," he said, "I've been doing some thinking myself, and I've decided to try not to yell at you anymore for leaving the water running or the lights on."

"Really?"

"Yeah. I've been after you ever since we got married and it's never done any good. I hate fighting with you about it, so I've decided not to bug you anymore. I'll just go around the house in the morning and make sure the lights and the water faucets are off."

"That's really sweet, honey. Thank you." I reached up to kiss him, deciding this was definitely not the time to bring up the fact that he'd left his socks on the floor for the 8,125th time—and the cap off the toothpaste. With my need for a hug and a make-up kiss more than fully met, I went back to writing what everyone tells me is a much-needed book.

Mixed Reactions

During the course of writing this book, I conducted numerous surveys and interviews with both sexes. The topic met with mixed reactions, and I had a lot of questions to sort through. There were times when I wondered if the book would turn out to be a comedy or a tragedy. For example, I met my writing friend Jane over lunch one day . . .

"Well," she said after our orders had been taken, "tell me what you're working on these days."

"I'm writing a book on what men and women need most in one another."

"Oh," Jane wrinkled her nose, "I don't want to read it. I'm mad at Peter right now, and I intend to stay mad." She hesitated a moment, then added wryly, "Why don't you make this men-and-women book a black comedy? You could call it *What Men and*

Women Need Most in One Another and Can't Get." Jane frowned and added, "Sounds cynical, doesn't it? Maybe I've been married too long. Do you think maybe I'm getting bitter in my old age?"

"Jane, forty-five is hardly 'old age.' And I don't think you're being cynical or bitter; you're just being realistic—and you've got a good point," I said, as I rested my chin on my hands. "In fact, every time I mention this book idea to friends who have been married for a while, I get so many laughs I feel like I ought to be writing material for Johnny Carson. One lady laughed so hard I thought she was going to need artificial respiration. After she calmed down, she said, 'I'm sorry, but it was either laugh or cry. I'm on my third husband, and I've yet to find a man to meet my needs. Take it from an expert—the chances of men and women finding someone to meet all their needs is about five million to one and getting slimmer all the time.' "

"That isn't really very funny, is it?" Jane replied. "I mean, it *is* one of those situations where you make jokes because if you didn't laugh, you'd cry."

Sadly, Jane was right. We laugh when we're really hurting. There are far too many men and women whose real needs are not being met. So in order to ease the pain they work at getting their mates to change—or they decide to change mates! In fact, I can't think of anyone who wouldn't make some changes in his or her relationship if it were possible.

Very few people can honestly say that they are satisfied with their relationships. Perhaps that's why so many move from one relationship to another in hopes of finding the one—that ideal someone, handpicked by God—who will somehow be the soul mate they have waited a lifetime for.

The issue involves all kinds of questions, including:

- Is there someone out there just right for me?
- Did I marry the wrong person?
- Is it possible to achieve satisfaction in marriage?

- How can I tell the difference between realistic needs and unrealistic needs?
- Which needs can I expect to have met in my relationship?
- Do I know the difference between my wants and my needs?

We'll be discussing all these questions and more in later chapters. But first I'd like to address a question raised by another friend, who by the way is happily married to her second husband.

Oh, No . . . Not Another One

"Why in the world would you want to write a book on men and women?" my friend Rose asked when I told her about my book. "The libraries are full of them."

"Because it's needed," I said. "Even with all that's been written, the problems are as bad as ever. If those books could solve all of our relationship problems, we wouldn't still have over fifty percent of marriages ending in divorce. If we have enough in-depth and sound problem-solving material on the subject, why are so many people unhappy in their relationships? I want to write the book because men and women are still struggling with interpersonal problems that leave them shattered."

"Okay, so the book is needed," Rose acknowledged. "But how is yours going to be any different from all the other stuff that's out there?"

"Well, for one thing, I plan to go deeper into relationship problems than a lot of books do. I plan to attack the problems from the inside out. Second, I'll be using fictional characters to dramatize my nonfiction themes and help readers get more deeply involved in the issues."

"Sounds intriguing," Rose said. "I think I'll read it, even though Stan and I don't have the problems you're talking about. You're right, though; there are a lot of broken relationships out there."

Many men and women who are fortunate enough to be involved in satisfying relationships might question, as Rose did, the purpose of another book on men and women and their needs. Yet I've had many more respond like Sharon, Kathy, Angela, Michelle, and Laura, who said, "Oh, I need that. When is it going to come out?"

Is "Happy Ever After" a Myth?

The high level of interest I've encountered in the subject of what men and women need in relationships corresponds with what I've read in many newspaper and magazine articles. According to columnist Ann Landers, living happily ever after is not exactly the norm. She claims that "for every twenty marriages, one is fulfilled, four are okay, ten are unfulfilled, and five are miserable."[1]

If this is true, then about 75 percent of relationships between men and women are unhappy. A couple of years ago, a book called *The New Hite Report, Women and Love* exploded on the market, claiming an even higher percentage of unhappiness for women. When asked, "Are you happy with the relationship?" a majority of the women responding to Shere Hite's survey said no. Hite tells us that 84 percent were "not satisfied emotionally" and 98 percent indicated they'd like to make "basic changes." Hite also reported that of those women married over five years, 70 percent reported being involved in extramarital affairs.[2]

When Hite's *Women and Love* book came out, newspapers and magazines everywhere questioned its validity. So did I—I thought surely her statistics must have been gathered somewhere other than planet earth. Were a majority of women really that unhappy, or did Hite just happen to turn over a lot of rocks to expose swarms of particularly miserable and hostile women?

Regardless of where Hite found the women she interviewed, one fact was clear. Not only were they unhappy; they were also *angry*—at men. And their barbs and arrows brought men to their feet with fists clenched, ready to defend themselves. Men and women across the country hurled complaints, insults, and accusations at one another. When the air cleared, it was evident that Shere Hite had told only part of the story. Apparently, men weren't any more thrilled with women than women were with men!

The Hite Report was only one arrow—albeit a deadly one—in the big quiver of book-weapons women used against men in the mid-eighties. Others included *Smart Women—Foolish Choices*, *Women Who Love Too Much*, *Men Who Hate Women and the Women Who Love Them*, *How to Love a Difficult Man*, and *No Good Men*—to name a few. Their message came through loud and clear: men are the problem, and if they want women to love them, they'd better change.

The "Bashed Male" Retaliates

One man, Warren Farrell, retaliated with an excellent book in defense of males, *Why Men Are the Way They Are*. He maintained that in truth women, not men, hold the power in male-female relationships. He asserts that our society has adopted a "new sexism," and illustrates by citing examples such as the book title *No Good Men*. Farrell claims this type of book expresses open hostility toward men, even though the author attempts to hide behind a veil of humor. "If you had a book called 'No Good Blacks' or 'No Good Jews' or 'No Good Women,' " Farrell says, "no one would tolerate it."[3] (I have to admit, the man has a point.)

Emotional bashing, whether directed at women or men, hurts. More important, it makes the road to reconciliation between the sexes harder to travel.

As I write at the beginning of the nineties, the hand-to-hand combat between men and women has settled into another cold war—probably because, ultimately, men and women need one another for survival. We are inevitably forced to make a truce—or become reclusive, single, and celibate.

But despite the lull, the battle has not ended. Out of the

chaotic whirlwind of carelessly strewn words, the rubble of broken marriages and fragmented dreams, staggers a steady line of wounded men and women who are becoming more and more disillusioned and needy. With all the advice we've gotten, our needs still are not met; we're still experiencing a high level of dissatisfaction and hurt. What's wrong?

What's the Problem?

Why is there so much trouble between men and women? I have searched for a label to pinpoint a cause: Feminism? Chauvinism? Stereotypes? Godlessness? Self-love? Self-hate? Pride? Lack of love? Sexual problems? Male-female differences? Society?

Perhaps all of the above—and I will explore these things in the chapters that follow. Yet I can't help but feel that the roots of our unmet needs go deeper than our differences—beyond sexuality, beyond men and women. Could it be that the depth of our pain lies in a secret place where no one—not friend or husband or even self—can penetrate? Perhaps deep inside each of us is a vulnerable, hurting person whose needs cannot be met because the protective walls we've built around that vulnerable self are too thick for even love to penetrate. We talk about having needs and wanting someone to meet them, but somehow we manage to find subtle ways to keep our deepest yearnings from being satisfied—or even seen.

I wonder if we aren't a little too much like soldiers armed for battle. We march through life, angrily crying for the other side to give up, yet unwilling to lay down our own weapons. We're like wounded soldiers hiding in foxholes—frantically firing away instead of crying for help. And I'm sure you'll agree that it's hard to help someone who stands firmly entrenched behind his or her defenses.

Love Is a Many Splintered Thing offers more than a bandage for those gaping wounds from the wars of unsuccessful relationships. You'll discover ways to dig deep, locate the source of the pain, and make necessary changes so that real and permanent healing can take place. It may hurt—surgery often does. But while I can't promise healing without pain, I can promise you that there is a Healer, a Peacemaker, a loving, compassionate God, who will gently and surely carry you to the other side of unhappiness and pain and give you a new spirit of peace and joy. What men and women need to heal their deepest hurts is a God who:

> . . . gives us hope in hopeless situations,
> And helps us see the rainbow
> On the other side of rain.
> He heals the thorn-infested wounds
> That we might smell the roses.
> And gives us tears to wash away the pain;
> Oh, but then . . . then . . .
> He gives us joy so we can laugh again.[4]

In my own marriage most fortifications have crumbled, some remain half-built (or half-demolished, depending on which side you stand on). We never pulled out the big guns of separation or divorce, but on the other hand, we would be remiss to claim success and marital bliss. Even though our marriage has, at times, been a major battlefield, and Ron and I both carry our share of scars, we see a lot of rainbows, roses, and laughter. And we count ourselves among the few "relatively happy" couples.

It's Your Turn

All in all, I've determined that I am somewhat happy in my relationship. Things could be better—in fact, I'm one of those women who would like to see some basic changes made. How about you? I've made some confessions to you and now it's your turn. How would you rate your relationship? Happy? Miserable? Somewhere in between? Personal Inventory 1 contains a relationship rating scale to help you pinpoint your attitudes. As you answer the questions, search your heart. (If you are not married, skip the ones that do not apply.) Base your response on how you really feel, not on what you think could, should, or might be the case. Remember, there are no right or wrong answers, because feelings are neither right nor wrong; they simply are . . .

Personal Inventory 1
Relationship Rating Scale

	Always	*Sometimes*	*Never*
1. Are you happy with your relationship?	☐	☐	☐
2. If you could do it all over again, would you choose the same person?	☐	☐	☐
3. Are your needs fully met?	☐	☐	☐
4. Do you expect them to be?	☐	☐	☐
5. Do you feel at one with your partner?	☐	☐	☐
6. Are you comfortable with your methods of communication?	☐	☐	☐
7. Are you satisfied with your sex life?	☐	☐	☐
8. Do you and your mate share responsibility in making your relationship work?	☐	☐	☐
9. Do you want your situation to remain as it is?	☐	☐	☐
10. Are you and your partner as intimate as you'd like to be?	☐	☐	☐

11. Are you committed to staying in your present relationship?

☐ ☐ ☐

12. Are you and your partner attuned to each other?

☐ ☐ ☐

Plot your answers on the scale below, placing a mark to indicate the intensity of your feelings. Then circle the area where most of your marks were made.

Never				Sometimes					Always
1	2	3	4	5	6	7	8	9	10

| |_____|_____|

The majority of my answers to the questionnaire landed between six and eight on the scale, which corresponds with my somewhat happy relationship. How did you come out? Responses falling largely in the seven-to-ten area signify that you are mostly happy. Five to seven suggests some dissatisfaction but indicates the relationship is workable. Marks primarily in the three-to-five range suggest serious difficulties. A majority of answers located in the one-to-three segment would probably indicate that your relationship is failing miserably. If these last two categories represent your relationship, I'd suggest invoking immediate rescue efforts by seeing a marriage and family counselor.

The questions listed above are only a sampling of what could be asked. Below you'll find some space to enter any thoughts, gripes, or problems that may surface as you consider your specific circumstances:

_____

_____

Another tool that may help you determine where you are in your relationship is to make a list of what you like and dislike in your partner:

Likes	*Dislikes*
_____	_____
_____	_____
_____	_____
_____	_____

These methods are not designed for compiling scientific data, but they may help you pinpoint specific problem areas in your relationship. Regardless of how long the lists are or where you rated your relationship, there will undoubtedly be areas needing improvement. (I can certainly think of a few in my marriage!) On the lines below you may want to list circumstances or situations that you see as needing to change:_____

_____
_____
_____

Later on in the book, we'll be looking at the prospects of making changes and solving problems in a way that will help us move into more healthy and satisfying relationships.

Coming Up . . .

And now I'd like you to get comfortable and turn your imagination loose. We're heading into the adventure phase of this book—the "fiction" I told Rose about. I've taken the liberty of booking you on a breathtaking, adventurous, tropical tour. As we move into the next chapter, our yacht, the *Kristiana,* awaits to take us on a fantastic South Pacific cruise.

Now I know some of you, especially if you're not fiction fans, may be saying, "Fiction? What's going on here? What's all this about a cruise?"

Before you get upset with me for sneaking fiction into a non-fiction subject like relationships between men and women, let me explain. No, I'm not a frustrated novelist. Nor am I living a double life as a romance writer.

The truth is I'm weaving fiction and nonfiction together for a very good reason. First of all, I've discovered that fiction can sometimes take us to places that ordinary writing can't. Stories can get us *involved* in characters and what's happening to them. Second, stories, like good illustrations, appeal to our emotions and imaginations; they make us *feel* what we're learning and not just think it. (Do you suppose that's why Jesus used parables so often?)

That's why I'd like us to take a cruise instead of just having a discussion. I hope the result will prove not only helpful but relaxing and fun as well. So with explanations and introductions made, let's look ahead to where our cruise will take us.

In Part 1, the first leg of our journey, we'll take a trip to the Fantasy Islands, where we can daydream about the perfect mate, dare to make wishes, create dream lovers, and consider what it might be like to have all our needs fulfilled and to live the "good life" we still suspect is out there somewhere.

You may still be protesting: "I don't have a problem with dreams and expectations. I'm a realist, so if you don't mind, I'd just as soon skip the fantasy bit. I've outgrown the Cinderella, Peter Pan, and Snow White syndromes."

But are you sure? You see, I believe all of us cultivate a secret garden in our hearts and minds—small scattered islands of fanciful thinking, myths, and dreams we still believe in—expectations we feel should and could be met, if only. . .

• If only we had more money, then we'd get along better.
• If only he would stop being so bossy, then I would be more pleasant.
• If only she understood me more, then I wouldn't need a mistress.

Perhaps you can supply your own list of "if onlys." No matter how self-assured and grown-up we think we are, we could all do with a trip through those places in the heart where we once upon a time believed that all things were possible, where our dreams really could come true if circumstances would change, and where all of our needs could be met if only the right person would come along.

So I urge you to relax and enjoy our sail into fantasy. Have fun and take advantage of the surprises waiting there for you. Soon enough—in Part 2—we'll wake up in Reality Land, where we'll uncover truths about unfulfilled expectations, changes that aren't made, lust, affairs, divorce, dashed fantasies, and shattered ideals. We'll also discover how past experiences and memories come back to haunt and inhibit healthy relationships.

In Part 3 we'll sail on to Reconciliation Bay, where we'll learn what our deepest needs as men and women really are. The needs we find listed there may be far different from what you might think.

Throughout our journey, we'll discover principles that can lead to restoration—to realistic, exciting, healthy, growth-enhancing relationships in which we can freely and thoroughly enjoy the men and women in our lives.

Part I
The Fantasy Islands

HAVE YOU EVER BEEN TO Disneyland or on a Caribbean cruise? Did you ever watch the television series "Fantasy Island" and wish you could make your own secret fantasies come true? Have you ever wondered what life might be like if you could discover your perfect mate? Well, in the next few pages you'll have a chance to sample the entire package.

Shortly, we'll be boarding an elegant two-hundred-foot yacht . . . no, let's make it a three-hundred-foot yacht. (Why scrimp on imagination?) Once aboard, we'll set sail for the Fantasy Islands. On the cruise, you'll enjoy the company of a party of fellow dreamers who, like you and me, are taking this tour in hopes of discovering what men and women really need in one another. A little later we'll even get a chance to put in an order for the ideal mate and consider what life might be like with the man or woman of our dreams.

In our sail to our island paradise, we'll sip exotic fruit drinks near the pool, dine with the captain in the lavish banquet hall, or simply lounge on deck as the sea breeze carries our worries far out to sea. Once there, excitement and adventure await us as the yacht's owner, a captivating man, guides us deep into the minds of men and women to discover what we really want from and for each other.

As we enter chapter 2, fix yourself a tall, cool iced tea or pineapple-coconut cooler, snuggle down in that easy chair, kick off your shoes, and turn your imagination on high.

As we step out of the real world and embark on our cruise, I'd like you to meet two of our traveling companions who are also making preparations for the sail. Read on and meet Samantha Jones and David Hartley, star-crossed lovers who just might remind you of a once-upon-a-time tale of romance in your own life.

Chapter 2
The Perfect Mate

SAMANTHA PAUSED midway up the block-wide marble stairs that led to a bank of glass doors. She moved to a nearby bench to rest. Not that she felt tired—Sam ran up those same steps nearly every day. But the thrill of what lay ahead on this, the fourteenth day of May—her twenty-fourth birthday—left her winded.

Sam ignored the irritating traffic noises and hints of smog, concentrating instead on the parklike setting designed into the building's entrance. Passing a blossoming gardenia, Sam paused to absorb the sweet, fresh scent of it. As she turned to enter the building, her eyes drank in the beauty of rainbowed crystal windows fired to an iridescent opal by the hazy morning sun. At the top of the forty-story structure overlooking downtown Los Angeles, Sam could see the penthouse windows—her office.

Sam paused to sit for a moment on the marble stairs. She smiled, closed her eyes, and turned her face to the sun. *What more could a girl ask for?* she mused. Six months ago she had created the most valuable tool of the century—a complete software program designed to provide men and women everywhere with the perfect mate. She had established a company and now, after endless hours of sales and marketing, she would have a chance to prove how valuable her system really was. Her dreams were finally coming true. There was only one thing missing in her life now—Sam wanted a man.

"Ah . . . excuse me," a deep male voice interrupted Sam's thoughts.

With eyes still closed, like a cat lazing in the sun, Sam responded with a sleepy "Hmmm?"

David's question fled from his mind and left him staring mutely at the enchanting young woman in front of him. He wondered what it would be like to kiss her awake—to take the pins from her upswept honey-brown hair and comb his fingers through its silken strands.

The hint of Polo® cologne drifted into Sam's awareness. She thought of *him*, her dream lover—the man her Custom Mate software would soon select as her ideal partner.

"Ah . . . excuse me, miss. Say, are you okay?" David lightly shook Sam's shoulder.

"I'm fine—just fine," she sighed, unwillingly withdrawing from her daydream. Her eyelids drifted open. "Oh . . ." Faded-denim blue eyes, sun-streaked sandy brown hair, chiseled features—the man looking intently at her bore an uncanny resemblance to the male image she had just conjured up in her mind. Samantha closed her eyes and opened them again slowly, thinking the man a mere figment of her overworked imagination.

"Oh . . . it can't be. Am I dreaming? You look like . . ." No, she was being ridiculous; she hadn't even entered her data yet. She jumped to her feet, only to discover she'd practically buried her nose in the guy's chest. Sam gulped and lifted her chin as she stepped back.

"Ah . . . I'm sorry, I was . . . thinking," Sam responded. "You wanted something?" A deep flush crept up her cheeks. Her mind bubbled with illogical thoughts as she found herself wondering, of all things, how it would feel to be held by those deeply tanned, muscular arms.

"Yes—I want you," David might have said, had he not been rebuffed by a shift of attitude that transformed her soft and sensual look to that of a brisk, career-minded businesswoman.

Sam consciously brushed away the romantic flutterings brought on, in all probability, by her silly, untimely daydream. Okay, so he was attractive. But Sam would not, could not, afford to waste her time on a man who hadn't been screened. If and when she did choose a man, he'd have to meet *all* of the criteria in her character analysis, not just have the perfect hair, eyes, face, body and . . . *stop that!* Samantha told herself firmly.

"I have an appointment at . . ." David said and stopped. There was no way David could tell her whom he had an appointment with—even if his association with Custom Mates had nothing whatever to do with dating. He'd been crazy to agree to fill in as captain of his friend's yacht. He was both an architect and a cattle rancher, and he had no trouble finding women on his own, thank you. Now, having discovered this tempting female, David wanted nothing better than to forget his appointment and set up another, more promising one. Unfortunately, he had already made a commitment, and since they were scheduled to sail that afternoon, David had little choice but to follow through.

The man was blushing. How sweet. Sam made a mental note to add *vulnerable* to her list of ideal male character traits.

"I was looking for Garden Plaza," he told her.

"You've found it," Sam said, pointing to the towering structure behind her. "Now, I really must go. I've an appointment in a few minutes." Sam turned toward the building and climbed the remaining steps.

"Wait!" David bounded up the stairs behind her. "Can I see you again? I may be out of town for a few weeks, but . . ."

"I'm afraid that's impossible," Sam said stiffly. "I have other plans." She turned again and hurried through an open door.

Sam wondered for a moment what it would be like to finally meet her ideal mate. Would he resemble the man she had just met? "I'll find out soon enough, won't I?" An unplanned grin spread across her face as she stepped off the elevator onto the mint-green and mauve carpet that covered the floor of her office suite.

In a few hours she, Samantha Margaret Jones, would be welcoming guests aboard Kansas Smith's yacht, the *Kristiana*. The noted actor/adventurer had told her that *Kristiana* meant "Free Spirit," and that was how she felt.

Sam had explained her program to Mr. Smith several months before. He'd been somewhat skeptical. No, that wasn't quite true. Actually he had laughed and shaken his head and said, "Miss Jones, I do admire your tenacity, but do you actually believe people are naïve enough to use a computer as a matchmaker?"

Indignantly she had confronted him: "Do you think you could do better, Mr. Smith?"

"Quite frankly, yes."

He must have changed his mind; a few weeks later she had received an invitation to be part of his three-week cruise. She would play a vital part in helping Mr. Smith's guests find their ideal mates.

Samantha picked up a folder from her desk. A David Hartley had been hired by the yacht's owner as captain. Since Mr. Smith would not be joining them until they reached Adam's Island, she had agreed to meet Captain Hartley to talk over details and handle any last-minute problems.

"Your eight-o'clock appointment is here," the intercom announced.

"Thanks, Gail, send him in."

Sam's office door opened. "Y-you . . ." she stammered.

The man filling the doorway exchanged his own look of surprise for a wide grin. He stepped forward and extended his hand. "David Hartley at your service, ma'am."

"Mr. Hartley." Sam responded with a brief handshake. "I

32

. . . I'm sorry if I seemed rude earlier, it's just . . . I mean . . .
I didn't realize . . ."

"It's okay." David's eyes twinkled as if he were enjoying
every agonizing moment of her embarrassment. "You had no
way of knowing who I was, and I have to admit I did come on a
little strong down there." He chuckled. "It . . . ah . . . looks as
though we'll be seeing each other after all."

"Yes," Sam agreed, smiling and thinking some very unbusi-
nesslike thoughts. Her very first cruise on Kansas Smith's magnificent, free-spirited love boat would be a pleasant one indeed!

Lofty Ideals and Starry Eyes

Let's stop here a moment to reflect on what's happening.
What we have here is a budding romance about to burst into full
bloom. There's just one problem. Sam and David are looking for
the ideal mate.

In case you haven't already guessed, Sam's business is akin to
a computer dating service. At Custom Mates, Inc., her clients
enter data about themselves and what they are looking for in a
mate. The computer then searches its data base and, depending
on availability, comes up with the man or woman best suited to
each client's specifications.

As the story indicated, today is a special one for Sam. Once
the *Kristiana* sets sail, she plans to enter her own data into the
computer. She has a long list of traits she wants in a man, and
she isn't about to settle for anything less.

Sam has been dreaming of this moment ever since age twelve,
about the time her mom and dad split up. She vowed never to be
like her mother and above all, never to marry a man like her
father.

We might laugh at Sam's insistence and determination to find
a man who wasn't anything like the man who married dear old
mom. Yet, whether we had a rough childhood or not, don't most
of us come into our young-adult lives with dreams about the kind

of person we want to settle down with? Perhaps we begin as Sam did, with high ideals and goals. We start out in hopes that we will find a true and lasting love and that somehow our most romantic dreams will come true.

He Was All I Ever Wanted

As I mentioned earlier, I interviewed and surveyed hundreds of men and women before writing *Love Is a Many Splintered Thing*. One woman, Jan, wrote, "At age twenty-five I had a list of attributes necessary in a husband. My friends despaired—surely Jan will never marry! My list of requirements were that he must:

- Be a growing, mature Christian.
- Be the oldest brother with at least one younger sister.
- Treat his mother and sister with respect and affection.
- Be at least as intelligent as, if not more intelligent than, me.
- Be creative.
- Be reliable.
- Be ambitious.
- Hold a good job.
- Be kind.
- Treat me with love and respect—with no insults or abuse."

Jan went on to say, "I met Mike. He filled the bill plus some, and I promptly married him three and a half months later."

Not everyone is as fortunate as Jan. Another woman, Sarah, said, "Sometimes when you're really attracted to a man, you think you see the qualities you want in him, or you might think you can change him. I married a guy who turned out to be insulting and abusive. At first I mistook Ted's aggressive behavior for being strong and masterful—I thought he was a man who could protect and take care of me. After we got married, his behavior wasn't 'noble' anymore, but I convinced myself that I could love him into a caring man. For years he had me thinking that our problems were somehow all my fault."

Sarah received counseling, but her husband refused to go for help, and he continued his angry, abusive behavior. A couple of years ago, she left him. "I still wonder how I could have made such a terrible mistake. I don't know if I'll ever marry again, but you can bet I have a long list of what I'd look for the second time around."

Sarah and Ted and Jan and Mike approached marriage with goals and dreams. For one couple the dream, for the most part, came true; for the other it fell apart. How have your ideals worked out? Have you found your perfect mate? And if you have, is your relationship happy and going strong? Or has it crumbled into ruins of unfulfilled promises and expectations?

A Cruise to Paradise

Whatever the current condition of your relationship, it's time once again to put reality behind us as we embark on our cruise to the Fantasy Islands. The sun is shining and a balmy ocean breeze caresses us with feathery fingertips. Romantic notions float in the air. I picture myself wearing a white cotton sailor dress with a navy collar and trim. The wind lifts my hat, and I hold it on as I wave to the crowd that has gathered to see us off. The yacht pulls away from the harbor and makes its way to the open sea.

After a few hours of sunshine, swimming, and getting acquainted with fellow shipmates, Samantha gathers us into the banquet room, where she gives us instructions on how to prepare the data for her program.

"Your first task is to think about what you want most in a mate."

A woman in the back raises her hand and says, "But I'm already married—what's the point in wishing?"

Why indeed? Yet, whether you've been married zero, two, five, ten, twenty, or even thirty-some years, whether you're divorced, dating, or engaged, it's never too late or too early to evaluate your relationships and yourself. Before unhappy relationships can be improved, we must be more fully attuned to what we honestly need and want—and also what we don't want. Only then can we realistically determine what, if anything, we can do to create more satisfying relationships.

Samantha passes around copies of a questionnaire (Personal Inventory 2) and asks us to choose the attributes we most desire in an ideal mate. I don't know about you, but I think I'm going to enjoy this.

Personal Inventory 2
What I Want Most in a Mate

1. If you could choose any physical attributes or character traits in the man or woman of your dreams, what would they be? Below you may check from the items listed or write in your preferences:

   Physical Attributes: Age _____ Hair color _____
   Eye color _____ Height _____ Weight _____
   Other: _____

   Character Traits: (You may find it helpful to mark each selection with a *V* for *Very* important, an *I* for *Important*, or an *N* for *Not very important*.)

healthy self-esteem	☐	committed	☐	masterful	☐
gentle	☐	fun-loving	☐	leader	☐
loving	☐	adviser	☐	ambitious	☐
kind	☐	trustworthy	☐	sentimental	☐
active	☐	assertive	☐	tender	☐
intelligent	☐	communicator	☐	amenable	☐
understanding	☐	open	☐	enthusiastic	☐
meets sexual needs	☐	agreeable	☐	fair	☐
good provider	☐	affectionate	☐	caring	☐
adaptable	☐	protector	☐	sports fan	☐

godly ☐ courageous ☐ intimate ☐
patient ☐ ardent ☐ supportive ☐
attractive ☐ virtuous ☐ romantic ☐
honest ☐ reliable ☐ creative ☐
gracious ☐ pedigreed ☐ passionate ☐
beautiful ☐ argumentative ☐ respectful ☐
good host ☐ confident ☐ self-reliant ☐
good hostess ☐ rich ☐ optimistic ☐
sensitive ☐ arrogant ☐ thoughtful ☐
good father ☐ well-groomed ☐ flexible ☐
good mother ☐ Christian ☐ confrontable ☐
nurturer ☐ realistic ☐ other:_____
sense of humor ☐ generous ☐ _____
adventurer ☐ even-tempered ☐ _____
faithful ☐ altruistic ☐ _____

2. Now, working from the list of traits you just checked, go back and circle or highlight your top ten needs and wants.

3. What qualities do you least like in a man/woman? List them below:

   _____   _____
   _____   _____
   _____   _____

4. Do you see any of those negative traits in the significant other person (if there is one) you are now involved with? If so, which one(s)?

   _____
   _____

5. If you could change any two things about the man/woman currently in your life, what would they be?
   (1) _____
   (2) _____

All done? Great. Samantha says she'll process our want list if we'd like, but I've decided to hold on to mine. I think I'll wait to see how the book turns out before I start thinking seriously about seeking an ideal mate via computer. You too? In that case, let's leave all this paperwork behind and move to the sun deck. It's almost time to sail into chapter 3, where we'll reach our first port o' call, Adam's Island. But before we go, we've still got time to soak up a glorious sunset and enjoy a relaxing evening in the yacht's spacious ballroom.

As we sail, close your eyes and picture the dream lover you just described. Look—there, across a crowded room. Do you see a stranger—or maybe a familiar face? I don't know why, but my dream lover's face is always that of my husband. We met many years ago, but I'll never forget those warm summer nights . . . he touched me and I heard music playing. His kiss turned my bones to jelly. There, with the moonlight transforming the sea to a million sparkling diamonds, fascination turned to love.

Ah, romance! Now you know my secret; I'm an incurable romantic. Oh, I know that every love story doesn't start out in a romantic haze. Some start out as warm, comfortable friendships, some as fights. But however they start, somewhere along the line love happens—and I think it's wonderful.

And speaking of love—let's look in on our reluctant yet hopeful couple, Samantha and David.

Sam waits expectantly for her printer to dispense the results of her character analysis. Finally, the verdict is in. But are we surprised? Of course not; we knew it all along. But Samantha, genuinely astonished, clasps her hands and twirls around the room. "It's him! It's him!" she shouts, then rushes off to tell David the wonderful news.

In the Stardust Lounge the band plays "Love Is a Many Splendored Thing." David and Samantha gaze dreamily into each other's eyes as the starry night weaves an enchanted web to lure them, with a magic as old as time, into the arms of love.

Chapter 3
Adam's Island and the Secrets of a Man's Imagination

IN THE LAST CHAPTER we left David and Samantha wrapped securely in the arms of love. Now, four days later, we find David at the helm, steering the *Kristiana* into her first port o' call, Adam's Island. David would have been thrilled to visit this place a few days ago. But that was before he met the woman of his dreams. All he's been wanting to do lately is haul Sam off to some private beach and kiss her senseless.

In the past couple of years, David had grown weary of playing the dating game. He was ready to settle down, but most of the women he'd met were too independent—too critical. It was hard to know what a woman wanted these days. If you opened doors, you were insulting her integrity; if you didn't open doors, you were insensitive and ill-mannered. A guy never knew where he stood. It had gotten to the point that he was afraid to smile at a woman in his office or tell her she looked nice for fear of having a sexual harassment suit slapped on him.

Sam was different. She appreciated everything he said and did. She was everything he'd hoped for in a woman—intelligent, soft, sexy, attractive, and caring.

"Hi." Samantha sauntered up to David's side and greeted him with a wide smile. "Isn't this where Mr. Smith is supposed to meet us?" she asked, shading her eyes with a hand as she perused the yacht-studded marina for a glimpse of him.

"He'll be along, but I wouldn't stand around waiting for him— Kansas blows in and out like the wind. But he always manages to show up in the right places at the right times. I'm rather anxious to meet up with him myself right now. Can't wait to thank him personally for getting us together."

"I'm sure he had nothing to do with our meeting, David. It was merely a coincidence."

"Maybe," he said, sliding an arm around her waist and pulling her against him. "But I'll be thanking him just the same."

Sam slid away. "Not now. We've got work to do. Do you think we should take everyone to shore?"

"No need," David said as he grasped her shoulders and turned her in the direction of the wharf. "Here comes our fearless leader now."

Samantha smothered a soft chuckle. "The guy certainly believes in getting into his part, doesn't he?"

And Samantha is so right. Kansas Smith stretches the limits of our wildest fantasies. In his movies he plays a history professor, but in my script, he's a wealthy adventurer who bears a strong resemblance to Harrison Ford, Michael Douglas, and Paul Hogan.

Dressed in a khaki shirt and shorts and sporting an Australian Akubra hat, Kansas greets us with a grin that would send an adolescent girl into shock. "Welcome to Adam's Island," he says in a resonant voice that makes every woman on board wish she could get lost alone with him somewhere along the way. (The men are just wishing he'd get lost.)

"As soon as you get your things together we'll go ashore. I've reserved rooms for you at Lancelot's Inn. While the men on board explore the grounds and settle in, I'll be escorting the women through some of the sights here. Women are not allowed outside the tour areas. It's a rugged place—what with the jagged peaks, canyons, wild animals, scorpions, and snakes. And ladies, you can look—but don't touch. That goes for the games as well as for the men. We'll be taking our tour shortly, so you'll want to freshen up. Wear something sporty. This is no place for women in frilly clothes."

He starts to leave, then turns abruptly. "Oh, and one more thing. You women are not allowed to take part in the political discussions. We'd rather not have to deal with our topics on an emotional level."

I stand staring after him for a moment, unable to believe I have just created such an arrogant, chauvinistic monster. I'll have to put an end to this macho attitude fast.

I catch up with Kansas in the lobby, barely taking time to notice the massive stone fireplace, rich mahogany woodwork and leather chairs, the forest-green carpet, and the books lining the walls. "I object to those remarks you made back there on the boat. It isn't fair not to let us give our opinions—or to let the men roam about as they please while we women are confined to seeing the sights you choose for us. And that remark about not touching—why, that's . . . Stone Age!"

Kansas bestows one of his warm smiles on me and melts a large chunk of my hostility. "Perhaps, but bear in mind, this is a man's world. Many of the activities men fancy are off-limits to women here on the island, and for very good reason. About the only place a man can have his private world these days is in his imagination. You wouldn't take that away from him, would you?"

"Well," I say, "I suppose not." I have never fully agreed with women who pushed their way into exclusive men's clubs. Oh, I realize that in some cases, particularly a few years back, these "men only" clubs excluded women not only from the facilities but also from important business dealings. And in those cases I don't blame women for demanding equal access. But generally, I feel men should be able to get away from women from time to time. I think it only fair that women and men be able to have private places where they can retreat apart from one another. "In fact," I tell Kansas, "I couldn't agree more. So Adam's Island is a men's club?"

"Of sorts, yes. But it's unlike any you'd ever find in real life. Here at Lancelot's Inn, for example, we have rooms and activities for men with every interest. There's a well-stocked library, a gaming room, a drawing room where political discussions and debates go on at all hours. The island itself is set up in sections. Section A is a wild-animal reserve where men can go on safari and hunt wild game."

"You mean they kill animals here?"

"Only what we can eat."

"Oh."

"In Section B is a fisherman's paradise with fresh- and salt-water fishing."

"But I like to fish—it's not just a man's sport."

"No, but it is on Adam's Island." Kansas surprises me by offering to carry my luggage to my room, continuing his explanation of the island on the way. "There are areas marked off for bikers, truckers, bowlers, and wrestlers, and soccer, basketball, and football players. All the sports a man's ever played or watched on television he can live out here. And to make the place a perfect paradise, every vehicle on the island is a four-wheel-drive truck with a winch."

"A wench?" I gasp. "You mean to tell me every truck comes with a female servant with cleavage?"

Kansas laughs so hard I'm afraid he will fall down the dark mahogany staircase. "Not a wench," he gasps as he comes up for air. "A *winch*—it's a power rig men put on their cars so they can rescue damsels in distress or pull cars out of ditches. A winch."

"Oh," I say. "It was a natural mistake, and I don't think it's the least bit funny."

Kansas doesn't apologize. He just drops my bags inside my

room and tips his hat. "Tour starts in thirty minutes, ma'am. We'll meet in the lobby."

"Wait!" I call to his retreating figure. "Just answer one question. Why? Why does a man fantasize about hunting, fishing, sports, and owning a winch so he can rescue people?"

Kansas pauses and scratches his head. "Well, ma'am," he drawls with a hint of a smile, "I reckon it's 'cause a man's gotta be a man."

A Man's Got to Be a Man

While I shower and dress in blue jeans and a light shirt for a strenuous trip through all-male territory, I remember reading some articles recently about how one of a man's greatest needs is to be allowed to be a man.

Men have changed in the last few decades. We've seen them adapt to women's new roles and attitudes. We've watched them sometimes freely, sometimes grudgingly give up what they once considered their territory. Women have pressured their way into even the most sacred men's clubs, jobs, and activities and urged them into the traditional women's realm of cooking, sewing, and nurturing children.

While many men have gained a sense of freedom in being able to enjoy changing a baby's diaper and playing peekaboo with little Claudia without feeling like a wimp, many men continue to struggle for an identity that separates the sexes and gives them something exclusively theirs. As Kansas said, about the only thing a man has that a woman can't invade these days is his imagination!

What Men Want That Women Can't Give Them

Most women I know want equality of the sexes. We want both men and women to be whole and self-sufficient, each able to survive without the other. And some have thought the key to this wholeness was for men and women to do all the same things.

We've come a long way toward these goals. Yet as writer Annie Gottlieb says in her article, "What Men Need That Women Can't Give Them," "The gains have been accompanied by a loss. There's something missing: a special vibrancy, vitality, gusto, pride, that we once recognized as distinctly masculine."[1]

In explaining the reason for this loss of vitality and distinctive maleness among men, Gottlieb says, "There is compelling evidence that what men need (much more than women, who seem to require less assurance of their gender identity) *is* a clearly defined difference between the sexes." The article refers to anthropologist Margaret Mead's 1949 book entitled *Male and Female*, in which Mead indicates that men and women can have all sorts of different tasks as long as men have their unique roles and women have theirs.

Boys will be boys and men will be men. And perhaps out of a need to maintain what they see as masculinity, men tend to turn to the very things women nag them to leave behind.

Some men fight—to save face, to defend their property, or to stand up for a true love's honor. Others watch and participate in sports, even though their wives may say they're being childish. "But sports, properly understood," says Gottlieb, "are anything but childish. They are ritual enactments of territorial defense through physical prowess . . . celebrations of masculine capacities that helped our species survive."[2]

When a man gallantly opens a door for a woman, is he being chauvinistic or condescending, implying she's too weak or stupid to open it herself? Occasionally, perhaps. But more often, according to Gottlieb, "He is making a symbolic statement that his superior physical strength will be used to assist and protect, not harm. . . . If they are not allowed to use [their physical strength] in a particularly masculine form of nurture, they feel useless, emasculated and vengeful."[3]

A Struggle for Identity

"Men," says Dr. Larry Crabb in his book *Inside Out*, "were designed to enter their worlds strongly, providing for their families, leading them (through servanthood) toward God, moving toward others with sacrificing, powerful love. . . . When Adam and Eve fell into sin," Dr. Crabb goes on to say, "they lost their relationship with God . . . lost the opportunity to fully enjoy all they were as male and female. For Adam, working now meant a battle with weeds and thorns, a battle he wasn't able to fully overcome. He became threatened as a man."[4]

Perhaps, then, a man's unwillingness to communicate from the heart, his escapades into adventurous fantasy, his shying away from what he thinks of as "feminine" emotions such as warmth, tenderness, nurturing, and compassion are, as Dr. Crabb goes on to suggest, the result of a "terrible fear that he may not have what it takes to win respect from her. . . . Men pursue defensive strategies for living designed to compensate for their lack of confidence. Some dominate their families and call it spiritual leadership. Others neglect their families in favor of the opportunity to make money. . . . The energy behind these self-protective maneuvers is tied to their threatened identity as men."[5]

A man needs a woman who can accept, understand, and allow him space to be uniquely male and who can help him accept his vulnerability so that he can pass through the fear and move into full acceptance of his God-given male potential.

The Land of Man's Imagination

My musings on maleness stop abruptly when I glance at my watch. I am ten minutes late. I rush down to the lobby just in time to see the last woman guest head out the door. I manage to catch up with them near the end of the path leading to a river.

"I was beginning to think you weren't coming," Kansas says as he gives me a hand into the wide tour boat.

"I . . . I was thinking," I pant. "About men . . ."

Kansas raises an eyebrow and gives me a sly grin.

"I wasn't . . ." I start to defend myself against his unspoken and totally erroneous assumption, but it is too late. He's already moved ahead to check seat belts and count heads. I really am going to have to talk with that man about his behavior. I simply cannot allow a character created out of my own imagination to get so completely out of hand . . .

The boat ride promises to be a pleasant one. We enter a thickly wooded area. Green leafy walls frame us in, and I can hear rushing water ahead. Suddenly darkness engulfs us. The gentle trickle of water intensifies to a deafening roar. The boat lurches, then plunges, leaving our stomachs far above us. I have no idea how far we've fallen, but within moments our boat has righted and is gliding smoothly through the water.

"By the sound of your screams, I take it you enjoyed your ride," Kansas says just as smoothly. His voice, even though I sense he is thoroughly enjoying our reactions, proves a welcome relief in the still darkness. I'm not certain where we're headed, but I have the feeling Kansas will protect us.

"Keep your eyes open now, ladies; we've just entered the Land of the Male Imagination. In the next few minutes you'll discover what a man really wants in a woman . . ."

A Tour of One Man's Mind

The boat slows and nudges the shore. A light gradually rises on what looks like a stage. A jungle scene comes into view, and before our eyes it turns from a still shot to a moving picture—animated with birds and animal sounds. A man walks into the clearing carrying a rifle, a camera, and a canteen. Leaning against a large rock, he wipes his brow and takes a swig of water, then removes his hat and looks straight at us.

"It's David," I cry. "What's he doing here?"

"He's fulfilling a dream he's always had to go on safari. Yet as you'll see in a moment, his mind is far removed from hunting wild animals. He can't hear or see you, but you will have the ability not only to hear what he says but to hear his thoughts as well."

As I watch David, his thoughts filter into my mind as clearly as if he were speaking. And those thoughts are all about Samantha!

She's everything a man could want, David's mind tells us. Intelligence—Sam meets that qualification and more. David winces as his thoughts roam to recall a couple of women he has dated. They were both a couple of sandwiches short of a picnic in the brains department!

David's ideal woman has to be attractive and well-groomed. And Sam is not only beautiful but also sturdy. He wants a woman he can hug without worrying that she will snap in two. Samantha is soft, with padding in all the right places. His thoughts move on in logical order.

He wants a woman who enjoys sex. Samantha told him last night that she doesn't believe in sex before marriage. He is pleased that he'll be the first, and he wants everything to be just right for her.

David's thoughts are heading for an *X* rating when they suddenly stop coming into my mind. "We'll have to take a brief intermission," Kansas says. "He's having some thoughts simply too private for others to be poking into."

"Oh, come on, Kansas," one of the women toward the front of the boat says. "We've seen TV shows that are more explicit than David's fantasy."

"Sorry," Kansas says. "I can't let you see what David is thinking right now. After all, this is a good clean book, and I'm certain the author wants to keep it that way." He glances at me and I nod my approval. "However," he grins defiantly, "there's nothing to stop you from indulging in your own fantasy."

The lights dim as he speaks, and I find my mind focusing on—you guessed it . . .

I recall a conversation I had with my husband awhile back about his need for sex.

The Need for Sexual Fulfillment

"How important is sex to you, honey?" I asked Ron, thinking to gather more data for my book. He had kindly assented to fill out the "wants" questionnaire, and I had noticed he had checked "meets sexual needs" as something he wanted but hadn't included it in his top ten.

"Well," he said with just enough of a smile to let me know it still had a high rating, "sex *is* important. But I think when some of the other emotional needs are met, sexual satisfaction will most likely follow."

My husband's response surprised me because I'd recently been to a marriage seminar and read a couple of books that listed sexual fulfillment as a man's first basic need. I was further surprised to find that only about 40 percent of the men I've talked with and who filled out the questionnaire listed "meets sexual needs" among the ten necessary elements in a relationship.

This came as a bit of a shock. I mean, after reading Joyce Brothers' book *What Every Woman Should Know About Sex*, I was under the impression that men think about sex about as often as they breathe. Dr. Brothers states, "Whatever a man thinks about sex, you can be sure that he thinks about sex almost constantly."[6]

Most men I talked with denied this. One man responded, "This is nuts. Even when I was eighteen and willing to mate with a department store dummy if given the chance, I didn't think about it all the time—it was more of a direct connection with other parts of me. . . . And now I think about plenty of other things."

I guess it just proves if you want to know what men really think you have to ask them.

Some experts, while conceding that sexual needs vary from man to man, consider sex a basic physical need. I don't agree with that premise, however, because a great many people (men included) choose to lead celibate lives—and survive. But whether or not we see sex as a basic need, in most cases, it can't be ignored by women who want to be the wives of happy husbands!

Personally, I've always enjoyed fulfilling that desire in my husband, though as I see it, he's satisfying me as well. Don't tell anyone, but I listed sex among my top ten needs! That's because I'm at an age where it's acceptable for women to think about sex as much or even more than men. Actually, I know many women at midlife (thirty-five plus) who want sex more often than their husbands. (We'll be talking about that later.) But I think women have always enjoyed sex as much as men—it simply wasn't proper to talk about it.

Yet even though many women enjoy sex, according to Dr. Willard F. Harley, who recently wrote a book called *His Needs, Her Needs*, most women aren't aware of just how strong the sex drive can be in some men.[7] Harley states that men often feel cheated because they commit to a marriage trusting that she will be "as sexually interested in him as he is in her. He trusts her to be sexually available to him whenever he needs to make love and to meet all his sexual needs." Harley also says that "a man cannot achieve sexual fulfillment in his marriage unless his wife is sexually fulfilled as well." In other words, a man would like a woman to satisfy his sexual needs. But perhaps he has even a greater need to satisfy her.

A Woman to Stand by His Side

The lights have risen on our stage, and once again we are privy to David Hartley's thoughts—more general ones now.

David wants a self-reliant woman, someone who won't be too dependent on him. Sure, he'll protect her and take care of her, but she has to be able to make decisions on her own at times. That's Sam—businesswoman, owns and manages her company—heck, running his quarter-horse ranch in Texas will be a snap for her. He just hopes Sam won't turn out to be *too* independent . . .

A hazy cloud of apprehension appears on the horizon of David's daydream. What if Sam doesn't want to move to Texas? David quickly dismisses the thought, knowing full well that when a couple marries, the wife goes wherever the husband's work takes him. He's seen his mom do it time and again. Yes, he wants a strong woman, but at the same time he wants her respect as head of the home.

He wants to marry a godly woman—someone who shares his spiritual as well as physical life. David hasn't asked Sam about her beliefs, but a gal as warm and sensitive as Sam *has* to be a believer.

His wife will have to accept and understand his goals and needs and be able to work with him and to believe in him. He wants a woman he can relax with and not play the hero role all the time. A scene from the night before drifts into his memory. In a rare moment he allowed her to see insecurity. "You know, Sam," he said as he leaned against the yacht's teak railing, "women like you scare me. You're a successful career woman. You see what you want and go after it. A woman like you doesn't need a man to take care of her—especially a guy like me. I'm afraid you'll wake up one day and decide I'm not good enough for you."

She sighed and wrapped her arms around his neck. "I'm so lucky to be in love with such a sweet, sensitive man. When you hold me I feel safe and secure. You're more than good enough for me—you're perfect."

But Sam is the perfect one, thinks David.

Of course, he wants his wife to have a sense of humor—he

needs a fun-loving gal who will enjoy horseback riding, hunting, camping, boating, and watching sports on television with him.

("The guy doesn't want much, does he?" one of the women sniffs haughtily, and a number of others murmur in agreement.)

He wants a woman who admires and respects him. Sam has told him he looks great in his white captain's uniform, and she admires his work as an architect. He hasn't had a chance to tell her about his plans to phase out his career as an architect completely and return to ranching full time. But David feels certain Sam will respect his judgment.

The Way to a Man's Heart . . .

David thinks it would be nice to have a gal who cooks even half as good as his mother. Sam has warned him that, except for creating a few specialty gourmet dishes, she has never learned to do much more than open cans. David, however, has decided that his mother and grandmother can brush up Sam's cooking skills in no time.

And she will have to be a good mother. He and Sam have talked about a family. She wants only one child. Of course, he is willing to settle for one at first. Then, when she's had time to adjust, he'll talk her into a few more. His Texas ranch house is big enough for ten kids, but he might be willing to consider four or five.

He stops to envision what his Samantha will look like pregnant with his child. Pride and joy swell inside him till he thinks he'll burst with pleasure. Uncomfortable with the swell of emotion his thoughts have invoked, David presses the image of mother and child from his mind.

While watching David's uninhibited display of emotion, I think how wonderful it would be if more men could relax and enjoy their feelings and openly share their innermost thoughts and concerns. I wonder if that freedom will ever come. I sigh deeply and turn back into David's thoughts again.

A worried frown comes over David's face, and his thoughts of what he wants in a woman are replaced with concern. Will he be the kind of man Sam wants? What type of guy does she go for? What if she decides she likes Kansas instead? Well, he'll just have to do whatever it takes to convince her that they have been made for each other.

I feel David's insecurity, his fear, and I don't want to intrude anymore.

The lights dim for the final curtain on David's thoughts, and I feel sad. I can see that he is heading for trouble and disappointment. He has high expectations. And while he looks tough and broad-shouldered on the outside, I can see all too clearly the vulnerability on the inside. I struggle with my feelings, wishing in a way that we women could see into all men's thoughts as we can David's. *But*, I wonder, *if men opened themselves up and shared their thoughts and fears, would we women still respect them in the morning?*

"I've only let you see a glimpse of how a man feels inside," Kansas speaks softly over my shoulder as if he had heard my thoughts. "Some women can't handle any sign of weakness in men. That's one reason it's difficult for a man to express his feelings."

"He wants too much," a female voice rings out in the darkness.

"Personally, if I were Sam, I'd look for a man with more backbone," says another.

"He sure is taking a lot for granted."

"The guy wants a robot, not a woman."

"See what I mean?" Kansas whispers to me.

I am disappointed that the women have spoken so insensitively. David was being honest; he deserves more respect. Yet I, too, have to admit to feeling uncomfortable. I grew up believing men are supposed to be the strong ones. Besides, his high expectations left me feeling a little insecure about how *I* measure up . . .

The boat shoots forward, and I sense a tension flowing from Kansas. "David doesn't want any more than most men his age. With years and wisdom, he'll realize he can't have it all, no matter how promising the package is to begin with." Despite his annoyance with the women, Kansas speaks in a smooth, nondefensive tone, and I admire him for that.

Thankfully, we've come out of the darkness and are once again floating along what looks like a peaceful river.

"Do all men want the same things?" asks another of the women.

"Yes, and how can we tell what men *really* want in a woman?" asks yet another.

"No, all men don't think alike, nor do they have the same needs. As for the second question, pinpointing specific needs in men can prove quite confusing."

How true, I think as I reflect on my own attempts to discover men's true needs, wants, and desires. At times I feel as though I am wandering through a maze. One thing is certain: not all men are alike—nor do they want the same things.

You might be interested in the results of my survey of men's needs, which are listed below. I don't consider my survey scientific, of course, but I found the results rather interesting and not really what I'd expected after having read several books and articles on the subject.

- Good mother: 70 percent
- Godly or Christian woman: 65 percent
- Intelligent: 55 percent
- Meets sexual needs: 40 percent
- Healthy self-esteem, attractive, affectionate, understanding, and caring: 35 percent
- Trustworthy and faithful: 30 percent

The men I interviewed came from varying backgrounds and ages, although the majority, about 80 percent, came from religious backgrounds. They were generally middle class but with diverse educational preparation. The list is read as follows: 70 percent of the men interviewed listed "a good mother" as one of their top ten choices, and so on . . .

Cutting Through the Confusion

Several years ago, when I first began gathering data for this book, I thought all I'd have to do was interview a variety of different men, ask them to fill out my questionnaire, read a few books and articles written by men—and I'd know precisely what men wanted. I tried to gather up the wants lists in a neat little package so I could say, "See, ladies, this is the list—this is what every man needs in a woman; if you want a happy husband, all you have to do is meet them."

It was not so simple. The more I researched, the more muddled the issue became. I finally came to the conclusion that men today are not sure what they want!

The Ever-Changing Male

Part of the confusion in determining men's needs is that today's men are in a fragile flux of change. Change comes as a natural result of growing older and (we hope) wiser. Need changes often go unrecognized, and unmet needs may be a hidden source of marital distress. I don't think I've ever heard of a man saying, "She doesn't meet my needs anymore." More than likely he'll say, "She's not the same woman I married." Changes in a man's needs come as subtly through the years as gray hair. The needs of a man in his twenties may be very different from those of a man in his thirties.

To see the ever-changing needs of men, let's get our minds back to our wild river ride through Adam's Island . . . oh, dear— I can see a tunnel ahead and hear the rushing of water again . . .

"Make sure your seat belts are fastened," Kansas says in his mellow tour-guide voice. "I know all of you women are anxious to know more about the changing needs of men so you can understand us better, right? So without further ado, let's take a ride into the seasons of a man's life."

Seasons of a Man's Life

All too soon darkness envelops us once again. Men of all sizes, shapes, cultures, and ages fade in and out as lights rise and dim.

"People are all different," Kansas begins. "And men are different. Consequently, men's needs vary widely depending on age, moral values, and cultural background. It's hard to keep track of these wants and needs. Sometimes men don't even know what's happening. We wake up one day and realize everything is changed. We find we don't want the same things anymore."

I understand exactly what he is saying. Until recently, not a lot has been written in the area of adult growth and development and the maturation process from young adulthood to old age. For years prior to the seventies, most people assumed that once you moved from puberty to adulthood, your personality, your needs, and your goals remained fairly stable until you hit the declining years. More recently, however, experts have mapped out stages, seasons, or passages that adult males move through which account for what at one time may have been considered deviant or unstable behavior. An example here might be a man who quits his job as a lawyer after twenty years to grow mangos in Hawaii!

Today we recognize that human growth and development is a continuing process from the cradle to the grave. And as I saw in my own surveys and studies, what a man needs in a woman varies with that maturation process. In order to understand the changing needs of men better, our boat will be taking us on a course through four seasons of a man's life. Here we'll see how his needs might change through each one. Naturally, not all men will experience the same sets of needs or changes. The scenes in this segment are based on my own observations, on psychoanalyst Eric Erickson's model of his life cycle, and on Daniel Levinson's theories of adult development, which appear in his book *The Seasons of a Man's Life*.[8]

Young and Tall and Tan and Sexy

Another waterfall. We drop with a splash at the bottom. After a series of sharp twists and turns, the river widens. A light mist hangs in the air. Apple and cherry blossoms drift down to greet us like pink snowflakes. Daffodils in full bloom line the shore. A man dances athletically down a flower-lined lane, clicking his heels and whistling "Singing in the Rain."

In spring a young man's fancy turns to love. At twenty-one, Jonathan's ideal woman is "really built—tall, slim, and sexy with a beautiful face." Research shows that typically males from puberty to young adulthood are walking hormones. Of course, as I mentioned before, not all young men view sex in the same way, and some object to statements that appear more stereotypical than accurate. One nineteen-year-old said, "Sure, I think about sex, but not all the time. I also think about cars, homework, my job, and food."

Men in their twenties are moving out of adolescence and into an early adulthood—their springtime phase in life. This is the time when they are establishing their male identity and planting their seeds for family and financial futures. They tend to be egocentric, choosing women who will bolster their egos and give them a sense of power, authority, and sexual potency.

He's Got Living on His Mind

The boat quickens its speed again, leaving the sweet-smelling spring behind, and heads into another stretch of darkness. As we round a bend, we see a golden cornfield and a young man examining a few quickly maturing ears of his abundant crop. In the distance, on a wooded hillside, sits a brick two-story home with white trim, surrounded by a split-rail fence. As the young man works in the warm sun, he sings softly to himself about summertime with its easy livin' . . .

Summertime might represent easy living for some, but it also represents a time when a man must care for the crop he's planted. The man in his thirties generally has settled into the early adult phase of his life and has shifted his focus from being part of his childhood family unit to establishing a place of his own. While men in this age group still see sex appeal and beauty as desirable attributes in a woman, they also tend to be more realistic—and more practical—than their younger brothers, particularly in today's economy.

Ben, thirty-two, says, "Providing for a wife and two kids is a tremendous responsibility, and I'm finding it both emotionally and financially draining. What I really need is a woman who will help carry the financial burden, or at the very least maintain a lifestyle compatible with my income. My ideal woman would be intelligent, physically active, hardworking, sensitive, loving, and committed."

In their early thirties, men have moved from establishing identity to a stage of what psychologist Eric Erickson called "generactivity," in which they generate interpersonal relationships and build families and careers. Ben would like his wife to be able to move with him and to be self-sufficient, with interests outside her job and home. He also wants her to be a good mother, a competent homemaker and cook, a fun-loving *compadre*, a communicative confidante (especially a good listener). He wants a friend and a partner—a woman who will help tend their fields.

Ben has high ideals and wants perhaps more than most women are able to give. Yet depending on the amount of energy he has left after working, he's generally willing to be a more supportive husband and father than he was in his self-oriented twenties.

And Autumn Leaves Start to Fall

The boat drifts lazily to the end of summer. Darkness, then light. Music fills the air, and I recognize the haunting melody of "Autumn Leaves." We see a gentleman wearing a Brooks Brothers suit, a picture of success, wandering down a tree-framed lane. He kicks a pile of leaves high into the air and watches as they swirl furiously, then settle to the ground.

As a man moves into his forties, the practical attributes he visualized in his hardworking wife often pale in significance as he finds himself facing another major transition in his life cycle— midlife. For a time, he may seem to revert back into the ego-centric, intensely sexual mind-set of the twenties. Bob, forty-five, planted a crop, tended and nurtured it, and is reaping the harvest. Now he's asking, "Was it worth all the effort?" "Have I succeeded?" "Have I failed?" "What have I done with my life?" "Who am I?"

In *The Seasons of a Man's Life*, Levinson writes, "As he attempts to reappraise his life, a man discovers how much it has been based on illusion, and he is faced with the task of *de-illusionment* . . . a recognition that long held assumptions and beliefs about self and world are not true." In this de-illusionment, Levinson says, a man may feel a tremendous loss or he may feel liberated—"free to develop more flexible values and to admire others in a more genuine, less idealizing way."[9] Bob is looking critically at the path he's taken and isn't sure he wants to stay on it anymore.

The midlife transition is often burdened by physical changes. Extra weight, shifting muscle mass, loss of stamina, and hair loss remind him that he's growing older. So . . . maybe he has put on a few pounds, and even if his teenage son beat him the other day, he can still run a good race. His golf game is improving. And he's still appealing to the ladies—he hopes.

Some men wander far off the path into the arms of those "ladies" to prove, as someone once said, that there's "a fire in the furnace even though there's a little snow on the roof." Some prefer to work things out with the women they married all those years ago, even though there may be little left of the relationship except a few lukewarm coals.

A man struggling through this phase wants a woman who'll understand his unrest, his insecurities, his questions and concerns. He may want a woman who'll be free enough in herself to escape to wherever his fantasies take him. He wants a friend and a lover. Sadly—and it happens all too often—if his wife can't change to accommodate his new lifestyle, he may want a divorce.

Dr. Lois Leiderman Davitz writes about this life stage that "inherent in the psychosocial dynamics of the average forties male is both the desire to jar himself out of a rut and the need to run to the warmth and safety of a stable marriage."[10] This can be seen in his widely contradicting list of wants and needs. The wife of a man in midlife may need to be adventurous and attractive but also warm, caring, gentle, affectionate, and forgiving.

His needs have changed and the woman who has borne and reared his children, and who is concretely set in her ways and in the security of her home, often ceases to be the woman of his dreams. Perhaps as the illusions lift, he sees with acute reality a marriage without love, excitement, or common interests. Autumn is perhaps the most difficult of all transitions for both men and women, and all too often it ends in a hard winter of separation and divorce.

In the Sparkling Firelight

Our ride continues through another phase of life—not quite winter. Instead of the frigid outdoor scene we expected, we see the interior of a house. The warm glow from its fireplace takes the chill out of the October air. A distinguished man with a streak of silver at his temples lounges in a brown velour robe and warms his feet on the hearth. He reaches across the sofa to take his wife's hand. Her soft, rounded face crinkles into a warm smile as she sets aside her papers and snuggles against the man she loves.

It's late autumn for a man like Cal, who is in his fifties. The chill in the air is lessened by a warm fire and a faithful, loving woman at his side. Ideally, he's adjusted to the new, liberated man and grown more accepting of his identity as a middle-aged adult. Cal wants a woman who'll be his companion and friend—a woman who is warm, comfortable, and caring. A young sexy chick probably isn't part of his fantasy anymore, possibly because he realizes his energies are better spent admiring a woman with inner beauty who is proud to call him a friend and with whom sex is a relaxing, fulfilling interlude of love and affection rather than a frenzied proof of manhood.

Younger Than Springtime

From the crisp autumn night and a fire's glow we move quickly through a winter wonderland, not stopping until we reach the end of winter and the beginning of spring. Bare trees line a snow-covered lane, and an elderly man carefully makes his way along the sidewalk. The sun plays hide-and-seek between cloud patches. The air hums with warmth of memory—and promise.

Bill is older . . . grayer; his memory isn't what it used to be, and neither is his hearing. But, like Maurice Chevalier in the movie *Gigi*, he laughs and says, "Am I growing old? Oh no, not me."

Once the seasons turn full circle, springtime comes again—perhaps not in the body but certainly in the mind. His life, although perhaps disturbed by retirement issues or illness and loss of family and friends, eases into stability. He becomes more content with life, perhaps because the only alternative to life is death. Coming to grips with his own mortality can release a man so that he and his life partner can settle into a relaxed lifestyle their children may refer to as a second childhood. (Of course, there's the danger of their children thinking they've become senile when what they're really doing is having fun. I recently saw a bumper sticker on the motor home of a retired couple that said, "I'm into heavy metal: my hair is silver, my teeth are gold, and I've got a lead bottom.")

At any rate, a man's desires have certainly changed at this point in his life. Now he's happy with a companion, a friend, a woman by his side who enjoys life as much as he does—one who'll stick by him in sickness and in health . . . till death.

A Need for Understanding

Obviously, not every male will fit into the seasonal pictures we've seen. Perhaps you recognized threads of your relationship woven through the fabric of changing needs, perhaps not. And maybe you are aware of sixty-year-olds who still struggle with identity problems, or men in their forties still struggling to build a career.

An important factor to consider, therefore, is that when people fail to grow and mature healthily through the various stages from infancy to old age, we encounter what might be termed developmental snags or hang-ups. For example, a two-year-old who never learned trust may grow into a thirty-year-old whose lack of trust borders on paranoia. Still, understanding the order of development in a man's life can help us understand better what men really need at any stage of life.

So, what *do* men really need?

Many men are talking more openly about their real needs these days. More and more they are coming out from behind the stereotyped male image of the he-man hero and telling the world how they really feel. For centuries men have been under tremendous pressure to perform in the way they think the women in their lives want them to.

As men talk about their various needs, they often express just as many fears and insecurities as women do. Men, simply because they are men, are not immune to cruel jokes and insensitive jabs at their masculinity. Men have desires, hopes, dreams; they crave the security of a warm, loving relationship, a home and family. Perhaps one of a man's most basic and vital needs is for someone to understand his struggle, his confusion, and his striving to meet the challenges of living as a man in a world where no one is really sure just what a man is anymore.

The Need to Be Accepted and Appreciated

A man needs a woman who not only tries to understand him but who also accepts and appreciates him. Over and over as I read articles about men and books written by men, and as I listen to men, I hear one very clear and distinct message: "I'd like to be accepted as I am—appreciated for what I do, not be rejected because of what I'm not."

Noted author and pastor Randy Alcorn shared this concern with me: "One thing that strikes me is the number of people, especially women, who have been to all the seminars, read the books, seen the films, and who know what the ideal husband is really like. Then they look at their husband, and he's a brute or a bore in comparison. Their lofty ideals raise their expectations and consequently their disappointment."

Randy's statement struck a chord in me. I have at times been one of those women who read all about how a man should be and have made those comparisons. Over the last few years, however, I've worked at accepting and appreciating my husband for his unique characteristics and positive qualities. The need for acceptance is especially great when men are experiencing the often confusing stage of midlife, when they are not so sure they can even accept themselves.

Ah, but our trip into the male imagination appears to be ending; I can see the dock ahead. I have time for just a few closing comments. What men want and need in women varies greatly with time, situations, development, and personalities. I suggest the best way for each woman to learn what her man needs is to ask him. See whether he agrees or disagrees with what I've written here. If not, make a list or ask him to fill out the questionnaire in chapter 2. You may be surprised at what you learn.

We've listened to men's most intimate thoughts and infiltrated the ranks of men's wants, desires, and needs. Later on, in Part 3, we'll be looking at some deeper, more vital needs. Now, however, it's time to hear from the women. As we move into chapter 4, we'll once again look in on our young lovers, Samantha and David. Then we'll sail over to Eve's Estuary and have an inside look at what women want in their men.

Chapter 4
Eve's Estuary: A Woman's World

As OUR YACHT winds through the laughable, lovable, scary, and exquisite Fantasy Islands, we find Samantha lounging on a deck chair soaking in the warm South Pacific sun as balmy ocean breezes cool her skin. Across her lap lies an elegant long-stemmed rose . . .

From under a wide-brimmed hat, Samantha admired the man at the ship's helm. Six feet, ruggedly handsome, sandy hair, a firm jaw, broad shoulders . . . she loved every inch of him. David was the most beautiful male specimen she had ever seen.

Oh, but the wonderful part was that Sam felt she could have loved him no matter what he looked like. She had long ago discovered you cannot tell the depth of a man by the breadth of his shoulders, and while those rippling muscles might be paradise to touch, a man was nothing without a tender heart. Sam recounted to herself all the wonderful qualities she had discovered in him. Except for a few minor flaws, David Hartley had it all!

That was saying a lot, because Sam requires a great deal of a man. In fact, you may think that some of Sam's wishes are as attainable as a bowl of liquid moonlight. But remember, Sam is in love, and we're traveling through the anything-goes territory of the Fantasy Islands. And you may want to keep in mind that sections of Sam's list matched those of many of the women I interviewed. You see, even those of us who have served time in reality are still turned on by a little romance.

Let's focus back in on Sam's thoughts as she considers all the things she wants in a man.

A Little Romance

I want a warm, caring, affectionate guy who enjoys candlelight dinners and walks in the park, she mused, *someone who isn't afraid of romance.* She rolled the long stem of the rose between her fingers and let the scent of its crimson petals fill her nostrils. Sam smiled as she remembered in vivid color the events of the night before.

After their intimate candlelight dinner, David had escorted her out on deck to dance under a million stars and a pale blue moon that was so full and translucent Sam was sure God had hung it just for them. They talked about friends and family, work and play, and she marveled at all the things they had in common. Then, in the middle of a waltz, he stopped and said, "I have a surprise for you." The twinkle in his eyes drew her into their mysterious depths. "Don't move," he whispered. His feather-soft breath against her cheek sent a delightful shiver down her spine. "I'll be right back."

Moments later he returned. In his arms he held a dozen long-stemmed red roses, and on top of them lay a small package nearly obscured by a cascade of slender strands of curled ribbon. "What . . . how . . . David, where did you get the flowers? We've been out to sea for days." Then she remembered. "You didn't . . ."

"I didn't what?" He grinned like a small boy with a giant-sized secret.

"The helicopter? You hired a helicopter to bring flowers for me?"

He nodded and handed her the package. "And that's not all. I . . . ah . . . hope I'm not going too fast, but . . . here, let me help you." He closed his large steady hand over her trembling one and opened the lid of the blue velvet box. Neither spoke as he lifted a diamond ring from its holder and slipped it on the third finger of Sam's outstretched left hand. "Samantha Jones," David said in an almost worshipful tone, "will you marry me?"

"Oh, yes," Sam sighed, and they shared a kiss that held the promise of forever.

Yes, this man would definitely fill her need for romance.

A Man to Talk With

Sam also wanted a man she could communicate with—a man who would share her thoughts, ideas, and dreams. David was the first man she'd ever known who would actually listen to her opinions and take her seriously. Too many of the men she'd dated talked mostly about themselves. For a long time she'd thought all men were like her father, who never listened but only lectured and yelled.

In addition to needing a man she could talk with, Sam wanted a man who would be honest and open with her. She prided herself on being a good judge of character. David's expressive blue eyes told her this man would never keep anything from her. Sure, he was a little reluctant and embarrassed about expressing his feelings, but marriage would open him up more.

Sam, perhaps because she had struggled so hard to improve her own sense of self-worth, wanted a self-assured, secure, motivated man with a solid career. She couldn't accept a man who felt like a failure because she made more money than he did.

David didn't seem to mind her career. In fact, he had been genuinely impressed when she told him what she'd accomplished. She felt sure he'd allow her to grow and develop without her success being a threat to his ego.

Cherish Is the Word

Sam believed a husband should cherish his wife. And only last night David had said, "You know, Sam, I think I know how thrilled Adam must have felt when God created Eve just for him, because . . . oh Sam, you are my gift from God." He traced the outline of her jaw and lips with his thumb and whispered, "I love you."

(Sigh. I can't blame Sam for falling for this guy. Fantasy or no, I would find a man like David terribly hard to resist. But then, as I've said before, I'm an incurable romantic.)

Sam wanted a passionate lover—one who met her needs for affection and sexual fulfillment. Although she was still a virgin, she'd read a few explicit novels so she knew pretty much what to expect—or did she? She shrugged off anxiety's caution. With David, every moment in the bedroom would be pure ecstasy. Hadn't they, in essence, been making love for days?

A Woman Wants More Than Romance

Ah, but Sam's mind was not filled only with fanciful thoughts about her lover; she had practical needs as well. David had talked about God, and that meant he probably had high morals. This was important because Sam wanted to be able to trust and depend on him. She had lived too many years with a father who promised the world and gave nothing.

The man Sam married would have to be a good father. She didn't want a man who'd spend his whole life at the office— "or in a bar," she murmured cynically, thinking of the life she'd had as a child. She wondered at times if it would have been better not to have a father at all. Sam quickly pushed the unpleasant memory out of her mind, thinking that David would be the kind of man whose family came first—a man she could count on.

Intelligence was a must in a man. She had a master's degree in business and education. They hadn't talked about his educational background, but Sam knew a person doesn't become an architect without having a lot of training! And he even understood computers—he said he'd learned about them in the navy and used them in his architectural work.

Sam wanted a man who wasn't deathly afraid of Windex®, dishwater, and vacuum cleaners. Since they would both be working, she wanted a husband who willingly shared in the household responsibilities. And David would, she was sure of that. She had seen his quarters on the ship and had been mildly surprised at how immaculate he kept them, especially since the only time they'd been separated on this trip was to sleep. And that, Sam thought dreamily, would very soon be changing.

Finally, Sam thought, a husband should be a soul mate. Already she could see that they moved to the beat of the same drummer. Sometimes without saying a word each seemed to know what the other was thinking. He loved poetry and sailing; so did she. Sam envisioned the fun they'd have together . . . quiet weekend mornings, breakfast on the patio of her Malibu beach house, concerts in the park. She saw them running on the beach together every morning, watching the sun go down every night. David and Samantha. They had each been only half of what they could be—like two pieces of a puzzle, they'd come together and would very soon become one.

Welcome to Eve's Estuary

Samantha's daydreaming halts abruptly as the crew scurries about making preparations to dock at the village on Eve's Estuary. She comes to stand at the railing with us.

How different this countryside looks from Adam's Island! The all-male island had a sturdy look about it—massive, jagged cliffs and boulders, with abundant plant life and waterways that balanced its rugged terrain. It was an island fortress, a place one could feel secure and protected.

The land around Eve's Estuary, on the other hand, lies open and exposed, with sloping hills and grassy meadows. Her multicolored floral fields and tidy village beckon us to enter the land and enjoy what it has to give.

Perhaps the terrain is symbolic of the way woman was originally created. "Women were designed to courageously give all they have (intellect, talents, wisdom, kindness . . .) to others in warm vulnerability, allowing themselves to be entered and wrapping themselves with supportive strength around those with whom they relate, offering all they are as female image-bearers for a godly purpose."

Larry Crabb wrote those words in his book *Inside Out*. It's a beautiful description, and I sometimes see this giving, loving womanhood, the essence of Eve, in some of my friends, who have found their place in the world and have come to accept themselves as uniquely created in God's image.

Even though we catch rare glimpses of Eve in people we know, sin has worked to destroy this image in women. Dr. Crabb goes on to say, "In sin, Eve could no longer count on Adam to respond to her love. The support and vulnerability through which she expressed her womanliness now endangered her. She had to become tough and hard in order to handle the reality that Adam was no longer a perfect partner. She became threatened *as a woman*, as a person who finds joy in accepting and embracing others but who now feels compelled to defensively control her relationships."[1] And that perhaps accounts for so much of the awkwardness, unrest, and misunderstanding between men and women.

As we approach Eve's Estuary, the welcoming landscape seems to accept and embrace us—men and women alike. So let's go ashore now and experience the sights and sounds. Perhaps in the process we can rediscover Eve and learn more about what women really need in men.

As we disembark at the village I notice that men and women have equal access to all facilities and are free to roam about as they please. There is less structure here than on Adam's Island. I find myself thinking about Kansas and wondering if he's planning a tour like the one he conducted in the last chapter. Since I don't see any men wandering around, I figure he must have started already. Too bad; the women might have enjoyed seeing how he handled the subject of women's needs. But it's just as well; we women have plenty to keep us busy.

At an information booth, we find brochures and booklets telling us of all the wonderful treats that await us. There is a colorful village shopping mall as well as bazaars, art shows, and classes in interior decorating, quilting, ceramics, and any kind of craft you can imagine. We could even attend a gourmet cooking class.

Of course, we could also scuba dive in the estuary, walk or maybe cycle along the waterfront. Or we could spend the day in one of the many beautifully landscaped parks and play tennis, golf, or swim. Personally, I'd enjoy taking some time to watch the children play—truth is, I miss my grandchildren. Maybe I'll even lie in the grass and look for cloud creatures . . .

And this sounds like fun! We could take an old-fashioned, horse-drawn carriage ride and a tour of elegant homes—maybe I could get decorating ideas for my dream house. Or we could charter a tour boat.

Eve's Estuary offers a choice of delightful restaurants. Maybe this evening we could get together for a candlelight dinner at Maxine's overlooking the harbor. Then later we can soothe our aching muscles in the Jacuzzi®—each hotel room has its own.

With my mind filled with ideas of delightful things to do, I hurry out of the information center, eager to get started on what promises to be a glorious day.

As I step into the street, I nearly collide with a man wearing Levis® and a khaki shirt, with a camera slung over his shoulder. "Oops—sorry, ma'am," he says in a familiar drawl as he grabs my elbow to steady me.

"Kansas," I say, "why aren't you in your tour-guide costume? Aren't you going to show the men around Eve's Estuary?"

"Me?" he asks. "Surely you jest. I'm a man, and the one common thread among men is that we have never fully understood women. This chapter is in your hands."

I start to argue. After all, he came out of my imagination and should know all about women. But alas, he entered the book as a man, so it appears I have no choice but to accept his role.

"But Kansas," I ask as he turns to go, "couldn't you at least come along—you know, for moral support. Who knows, maybe you'll discover what women really need in men. I mean, you do want to know, don't you?"

Obviously reluctant, Kansas stammers, "Ah . . . I'd like to, but I . . . well, there's a baseball game on in a few minutes and . . ."

"And you want to watch the game?"

"Yeah, some of the guys and I thought . . ."

I sigh and turn away without waiting for the rest of his response. I feel completely rejected. I mean, it's one thing for a husband to prefer watching a game (which mine did) to reading books like *What Wives Wish Their Husbands Knew About Women*.[2] But for your own character to turn on you. . . . Shaking my head, I start to walk away.

Kansas must have sensed my disappointment. "Look," he says, "why don't you wander around the shops for a while. I'll catch up with you later."

"Sure," I manage a smile. "Oh—and Kansas, do you suppose you could convince some of your buddies to join us? It's difficult to be a tour guide when you don't have an audience." I nod toward the crowd of men and a smattering of women who have gathered inside a furniture store, their attention focused on a bank of television sets. A loud cheer erupts.

Kansas strains to get a look at the action. He turns back toward me and I can see what it is costing him to remain civil. "Um . . . I'll see what I can do," he says, then quickly loses himself in the crowd.

I might have known. Leave it to a man to find the town's only selection of television sets to watch a game. I know—not all men are like that, and I shouldn't complain. At least Kansas agreed to join us later. When I asked my husband if he wanted to read this chapter to better understand women's needs, he said, "Not really." Unfortunately, I know a lot of other men who feel the same way.

Why? Most women I know are eager to learn about men's needs. Perhaps what women really need is for men to *want* to listen as we tell them what we need! But I suppose there's no sense fussing about it. Besides, there's hope on the horizon. Kansas is willing . . . no, scratch that . . . he's *agreed* to listen to women talk about what they want and need in men.

Since I'm stuck as a tour guide with no men to guide, I might as well share some interesting discoveries I made while going over the women's questionnaires and interviews. We can talk about it as we browse through the village mall.

What Do Women Want?

In the first few pages of this chapter, Sam told us what she wanted in her man. Maybe some of you saw her ideals as lofty, unattainable, and unrealistic. Perhaps they are, but remember that Sam's wants and desires are being viewed through shades of romance, moonlight, and roses.

You might be interested in seeing what other, perhaps more "down to earth," women want from the men in their lives. The women I interviewed are ages twenty-two to fifty-eight and come from middle-class families of varied backgrounds. About 50 percent are married, 25 percent are divorced, and 25 percent are single. Their opinions are listed below:

- High self-esteem or self-worth: 80 percent
- Godly or Christian man: 72 percent
- Good father and a communicator: 64 percent
- Intelligent and loving: 52 percent
- Meets sexual needs and has a good sense of humor: 48 percent
- Affectionate and reliable: 40 percent

As you can see, the most frequently checked attribute that women want in men is *high self-esteem*.

"I want a man who is self-sufficient," one woman wrote, "one who doesn't need me in order to feel fulfilled."

Another wrote, "I want him to feel good about himself and not be threatened by my accomplishments."

I chuckled as I noticed that a good sense of humor ranked up there with sex. And speaking of sex, did you notice that more women than men rated "meets sexual needs" among the top ten needs—48 percent as compared to 40 percent? Ver-r-ry interesting.

Even though my survey clearly showed some needs as ranking higher than others, I hesitate to use this list to establish criteria of what all women want. My list simply tells me what the women I surveyed wanted. Your opinion may be entirely different. As we'll see all the way through this chapter, women's needs and wants are closely tied in with who we are and what we've been through, not to mention where we are at the moment.

For example, I asked my friend Dana, who had recently lost her husband through divorce, what she wanted in a man, and she said, "Oh boy, you mean I get to choose?"

"Of course. This is a fantasy."

"Let's see . . . respect. Yes, without respect there is abusive behavior. I want . . . no, I *deserve* someone who respects every part of me—my creativity, my intelligence (he listens when I share my opinions), my imagination (he doesn't ridicule me), my space, my feelings (he doesn't laugh at my fears or tears)."

"You feel very strongly about this, don't you?"

"You bet I do. I had a husband who had no respect for anyone, especially me. I can't believe I lived for so many years with that man. But I didn't know. I guess because I was brought up in an abusive home, I saw his behavior as normal."

Dana's life experience, her pain, has a great deal to do with how she prioritizes what she needs and wants in a man.

The Ultimate Sacrifice

"I see you're doing well without me." A deep and by now recognizable voice interrupts my train of thought.

"Why, thank you, Kansas. I'm glad to see you acknowledge that a woman *can* function without a man. However, I have to admit the chapter is more fun when you're in it. You add a sense of—I don't know—adventure, maybe. And by the way—that baseball game sure didn't last long."

"It isn't over," he says ruefully. "I left in the middle of the fifth inning when my conscience kicked into high gear and I felt guilty leaving you alone in this. Besides, maybe this stuff could help me with my own relationship—that is, my future relationship."

"Oh." I don't know what to think. Imagine a man giving up a major sporting event to talk about women's needs . . . of course, the man had been born of my imagination, but even so, think of the sacrifice! I realize that not all men are sports fanatics, but from my viewpoint, this truly is a trip to the Fantasy Islands.

"You're alone," I observe. "The others wouldn't come? Why?"

Kansas rakes his fingers through his hair. "Are you sure you want to know? You're not going to like the answer."

"I'm a counselor, Kansas," I say firmly. "It's my job to understand people and accept them—even men."

"Okay." He pauses. "The men I talked to said they'd like to know about women's needs. But they felt there wasn't much point in coming because when it comes down to basics, women really don't know what they need. They give too many mixed messages, and . . . well, the fact is, the men I talked to said that women are just too darn hard to please."

Kansas must see steam escaping from the top of my head because he immediately raises both hands in a gesture of surrender. "Now wait a minute. Before you say something you'll regret, hear me out. I'm being honest with you—the least you can do is look at this objectively."

"I know exactly what I want in a man!" I sniff indignantly. "And I do not send mixed messages."

"Maybe you don't, but there are a lot of women who do. How's a guy supposed to know what women want when they all seem to want different things?"

"I . . . I guess I need to think on this one awhile, Kansas," I concede. "Why don't you go on back to the game? You could join me later."

His smile spreads clear to his ears. "Right. Thanks. Oh, and I'll see what I can do about talking some of the guys into coming." He tips his hat and races off in the direction of the furniture store.

As I think about what Kansas reported, I begin to see his point. In today's society we see a wide array of women's views and issues: liberal; conservative; militant feminists; gentler, kinder feminists; and antifeminists. Some of these women have a clear vision of their needs while others do not. Still others feel they have no needs at all where men are concerned.

Women Who Don't Need Men

I can understand why men might be reluctant to explore the area of women's needs. Being under attack by some of the more militant women's groups would make anyone—man or woman—a little gun-shy. In fact, there's even a group of these women here. They own and operate a T-shirt shop right here in the village square. They've been protesting the acceptance of men on the island and have led a movement to have all men banned. Of course, not all women who don't need men are that militant or bitter. Many express a subtle "who needs men" attitude, often because they've experienced unhappy relationships and may not want to risk getting involved again.

For example, when *The New Hite Report* came out, newspapers across the country went wild printing responses from readers. One twenty-seven-year-old single woman wrote (and many others echoed her sentiments), "I gave up on men several years ago, because they're not worth the effort. For what little men are capable of or willing to give in a relationship, they're not worth the emotional, spiritual, financial, physical, etc. etc. effort. I receive more friendship and support from my cat. (And he doesn't leave the toilet seat up.)"[3]

While I'm not ready to give up on men, I do understand that woman's point of view. I'm fortunate in having a husband, who, though not perfect, loves me and is committed to our marriage. He also gives of himself and expends as much energy as I do to keep our relationship growing and alive. I love my husband. And yet, if anything ever happened to Ron, I'm not sure I'd want to invest the time and effort to become intimately involved with another man.

Women Who Don't Know What They Want

Kansas said women want too much and that we're not sure what we want. Maybe he was partly right. At least I can see how men might get that impression. If I were young and single again and could know what I know now, my want list might look like this: I'd look for a man who is warm, caring, romantic, and willing to come home from a hard day at the office, cook a five-course meal, do a load of laundry, and dust—all before watching the evening news. I'd be thrilled if he came equipped with a social conscience that fully understood and opposed the oppression of women throughout the ages and swore I would never be tyrannized as long as he was around. I'd also like him to be strong, protective, able to leap tall buildings in a single bound—just kidding about the tall buildings . . .

"Well, here we are," Kansas' baritone voice breaks into my fantasy about the ideal man. "Tell us what women want."

I turn my brightest smile on the handful of men with Kansas and say, "I'll be happy to. But first, I'd like you to clarify something for me. Kansas told me one of the reasons you didn't especially want to explore the area of women's needs was that you think we send mixed messages. Could you explain that?"

A distinguished, balding gentleman in a brown tweed suit clears his throat and speaks. "Women say one thing and show another. They read millions of romance novels every month, and in every book some broad-shouldered, slim-hipped hero carries his 'lady' off to some love nest where they'll live happily ever after."

"Yeah," a well-muscled man in jeans and sleeveless black T-shirt adds. "And when you got a build like Superman, or act like you think heroes act, they tell you you aren't sensitive or vulnerable enough. I'm tired of playing games and trying to figure out who wants what. You try to change and be what a woman wants you to be, and then she dumps you for someone entirely different. Why can't women make up their minds what they want so we can settle this nonsense once and for all?"

"Are you saying that men would like to be what women want them to be, but they haven't been able to figure us out yet?"

"I think that sums it up," Kansas says.

"Kansas here says you'll tell it to us straight—that right?" a tall guy with thick curly black hair and Paul Newman eyes asks.

"Ah . . . right." I laugh nervously and look at Kansas. He just smiles and tips his Australian hat a little lower on his forehead, enjoying my dilemma. What can I say? You see, if these men are right, I'm one of those women sending mixed messages. I do like tender, sensitive, vulnerable men. But I also like the strong, powerful, take-charge type of hero.

Is it any wonder men are left standing on the sidelines trying to discover who and what they are and what women really want? It's a crazy, out-of-control world where men are told macho isn't cool, but see that it's guys like Rocky, Indiana Jones, and Crocodile Dundee who wind up with the cute chicks. No wonder learning what women really want is about as tricky as growing palm trees in Alaska.

It looks as though women do, at times, send mixed messages and that this produces confusion among men as to what today's woman wants in today's man. But as I recall, men aren't exactly sure what they want, either.

Women Who Want Too Much

Then there's the accusation that women want too much. Is this true, or are men just looking for excuses to keep from giving up ground they thought was theirs or from accepting more responsibility?

What a dilemma we face! Do we place the blame on women, men, or both? I look at my most important wants and needs, and I know many other women agree. We want to be loved, valued, respected, and treated as equals. We don't want to be controlled, abused, or considered inconsequential. Perhaps it is with these issues—especially equality—that the difficulties really begin.

In recent years women all over the world have taken a stand against oppression. We have fought long and hard to take ground that we felt was inherently ours. Some women pushed too hard and too fast. Large numbers of men refused to bend—refused to give up the control and power they thought was theirs. As a result, many of the alliances between men and women were shattered. As we search through the rubble of ravaged relationships, we all too often uncover wounded soldiers—men and women, victims of a war that perhaps could have been won by love rather than hate, by gentle nurturing rather than by fists and barbed words.

Do women want too much? Perhaps some do. But to attach blame on women is a cop-out. It appears to me that too often, both men and women want much more than the other sex can or is willing to give.

I've been silent a long time. I look back at the men.

"Looks like you've come to a conclusion," Kansas says.

"Yes, and I don't think you're going to like it."

"You might be surprised." Kansas tips his hat back and offers me a knowing smile.

"Maybe the message is confusing," I address the group, "and maybe some women want too much. But honestly, now, think about your own wants. Maybe you men are guilty of expecting too much as well. Don't you give mixed messages, too? We saw in the last chapter that men don't always know what they want, either. Why should women be any different? I do know that for the most part women are willing to learn about men. Maybe it would help if more men spent time learning about women."

A Woman's Changing Needs

The only response comes from a few men clearing their throats and scuffling their feet—I've hit a nerve.

"Women's needs do vary," I go on, "depending on personality, social status, political persuasion, past experience, and even hormone level."

In the last chapter we saw how men's needs change as they navigate through the life cycle. Women can expect shifts in their attitudes at various life stages as well, but for many women the scene is complicated by severe fluctuations during a single month.

In a book I coauthored entitled *Emotional Phases of a Woman's Life,*[4] Jean Lush and I showed how hormonal changes can affect a woman's emotional stability in both her monthly cycle and her life cycle.

Along with monthly fluctuations of mood, women experience stages of growth and development much as men do. In *Emotional Phases of a Woman's Life,* Jean Lush and I also discussed the various stages women go through, such as the:

- romantic phase, which covers women from about twenty-five to thirty-five years of age. This phase is not romantic in the sense that women who are in it think all is right with the world, but that they often tend to hold on to romantic or idealistic dreams.
- midlife malaise, which covers ages thirty-five to forty-five. During this period, marriage and/or career have settled into routine, and many women begin to question their life choices. There is often an emotional turmoil that accompanies midlife—a need for self-fulfillment, a yearning for romance, struggles with the emptying nest, and so on.
- menopause, and postmenopause, when our reproductive systems close up shop and leave us free for new challenges. Menopause is a difficult time for some women, but it is another step toward maturity and can be a passage which brings us closer to God.

What all this boils down to is that if you want to know what a woman needs at any given time . . . ask her. Bear in mind, of course, that she might not always be able to tell you.

What *I'd* like, throughout my monthly and life cycle, is a man brimming with flexibility and understanding. Above all, I'd want one who wouldn't divorce me because I'm having one of my bad days . . . weeks . . . months . . . years. I, in turn, would put up with all his changes!

Leaving Fantasy Behind

We've touched on some of the more expressed needs of women, needs that can vacillate from week to week. We've thought about all those things men and women want in each other and the changes we'd like to make. As we spend our final moments in the Fantasy Islands, let's bid a fond farewell to swaying palms, blissful nights, and ideal lovers especially designed to meet our every need.

Our farewell party takes place on the Isle of Lasting Love. Sunlight filters through giant shade trees onto a romantic garden. In a sparkling white gazebo trimmed with floral garlands, David and Samantha stand on a pedestal frosted in pink and white rose petals. Samantha is dressed in white lace, silk, pearls, and sequins; he wears a sky-blue tuxedo that sets off his eyes. Cascades of pastel ribbons sway like willows in the wind.

The preacher pronounces them man and wife. Tears stain our cheeks as they kiss, then scurry down the flower-lined path and up the boat ramp. We follow the happy couple back to the ship for an elegant brunch.

Some of us hurry, eager to set sail for Reality Straits, where illusions and myths encounter the facts of life. Others of us pause to wipe the lingering wetness from our eyes—knowing full well what lies ahead, yet hoping perhaps this time things will be different. Isn't it possible that this marriage, bathed in moonbeams, rainbows, and laughter, will escape reality's *deillusionment?*

Part II
Reality Straits

In exploring the Fantasy Islands, we discovered much about men and women and their needs. But fantasy is behind us now, and we're on a collision course for Reality Straits. Here we'll uncover the naked truth about high expectations and ideal mates. This is where fairy tales face the brutal cross-examination of real life.

In the next few chapters we'll identify various species of personalities and learn why some of us bloom with confidence while others wilt under the burden of low self-esteem. We'll dig among the archeological ruins and fossilized formations of family patterns that contribute to the many difficulties plaguing relationships today.

Reality isn't an easy place to be, but it's a world we must conquer and eventually learn to love. For here, among the jagged rocks of pain and suffering, we will forge the healthy attitudes that grant us entry into the healing harbors of Reconciliation Bay.

Chapter 5
Wishes, Falling Stars, and Dreams That Don't Come True

Twilight escorts the *Kristiana* into Reality Straits, then fades into the storm clouds on the horizon. A brooding dusk hovers over the churning charcoal sea, obscuring the entrance of the narrow waterway. Waves crash against the mammoth cliffs that lurk behind the mist like prehistoric dragons stalking their prey. Still. Silent. Watching. Waiting for the craft to shred its keel on their spiny coral scales concealed beneath the water's surface.

David shudders at the prospect of navigating the treacherous passageway with a stormy night as a companion. "Drop anchor," he calls to the midshipman on the aft deck. "We'll spend the night in open waters."

I breathe a heavy sigh.

"You seemed relieved," Kansas says as he moseys up to the railing.

"I am. I know those creatures out there are only rocks, but I'll feel much better facing them in daylight."

"Yes," he agrees, sweeping his arm dramatically through the air as though he were reciting lines from a Shakespearean play. "Creatures of the night fade with reality's dawn. But when our fantasies of evil are brought into the light, so also are our dreams and expectations of an ideal life." He grasps the rail and looks at me, moonlight reflecting the twinkle in his chocolate-brown eyes. "Are you ready to have your fantasies exposed?"

I'm not sure. But as I think of the fairy tales I've known, I can see that even in their glory they are laced with reality.

Perhaps the Cinderella story tries to warn us of that when, at the stroke of midnight, the coach mutates back into a pumpkin. Cindy, once belle of the ball, returns to scrubbing floors and waiting tables, and the magnificent white horses return to their mundane lives as ordinary mice. One wonders if the story should have ended there rather than leading us on to believe that for every woman there is a charming prince who holds a glass slipper.

What a shock it must have been for poor Cindy to watch the midnight hour strip her world of magic. Though Cinderella's story is a fairy tale, I can think of a great many real people who have found themselves caught up in an aura of enchantment, only to have time and truth whisk it away.

Ah, but enough daydreaming. It's time to return to our unfolding story of David and Samantha Hartley, who are facing the loss of infatuation's magic spell.

Trouble in Paradise

After securing the ship for the night in the Sea of Disappointment, David shrugged off the foreboding that had followed him all day. He hadn't expected the storm on the horizon, any more than he'd expected a squall to rise in his relationship with Samantha.

"David," Kansas laid his hand on David's shoulder. "You look a little down."

"It shows, huh?"

"Did you and Samantha have a fight?"

"You might say that."

"Well, conflicts are inevitable in marriage. I'm sure you two will patch things up. I've never known a couple more ideally suited."

"Yeah. I hope you're right." David ambled back to the honeymoon suite he had shared with his bride of three days. He wrapped his hand around the doorknob and hesitated. *Should I try to talk with Sam*, he wondered, *or just pretend I don't see that she's upset? Maybe I should spend the night in my old quarters.* He didn't want another encounter like the one they'd had this morning. Sam had grown increasingly sullen since their marriage. "What's wrong, honey?" he had asked. "You look unhappy. Is it something I've done?"

Sam looked at him a moment and sighed. "No, David, of course not. I guess it's just the letdown—you know, from the wedding and all."

David sensed she wasn't being honest with him. "It's me, isn't it? Tell me the truth. I'm doing something that really bugs you . . . you're disappointed in me, right?"

"N-no," Sam stammered. How could Sam tell him the truth: that she had been disappointed—no, devastated—with his idea of lovemaking. She had envisioned long evenings of kissing and talking and making love over and over until dawn—as it happened in the books she had read. Instead, it had lasted ten minutes . . . *ten minutes*! And then he had taken a shower, given her a kiss, turned over, and gone to sleep, leaving her empty and lonely. Maybe her mother had been right after all when she said that sex isn't all it's cracked up to be. "I . . . oh, Mother was right, men just don't . . ."

"Don't what?" The moment he heard his voice and saw the startled look in Sam's eyes, he knew the words had come out too strong, too harsh, but it was too late to pull them back.

Tears spilled down Sam's cheeks, and David pulled her into his arms. "I'm sorry," he said gently. "I didn't mean to raise my voice. It's just that I want you to be happy."

"It's nothing. Honestly, I'm fine, David." Sam sniffled, then

87

smiled and slipped her arms around his waist. "I told you, it's the postwedding blues. I'm just tired."

After a lingering kiss, David had left her to attend to his duties on deck. He hadn't had time to pursue the discussion—not if they wanted to reach Reality Straits by nightfall. Feelings of inadequacy tormented him, made all the worse when Sam didn't show up on deck all day. Was she avoiding him? Worried that their beautiful love affair was already ending, he determined to try all the harder to learn what he could do to make her happy.

Annoyance filtered in and mixed with his insecurity. It wasn't all his fault. Sam might be happier if she stopped moping around and cleaned the suite. He'd waited for years to have a wife so he wouldn't have to clean anymore.

Now, with the ship secured and the day ending, he could deal with Sam, and then, he hoped, they could get on with their lives. David hated loose ends. The doorknob turned in his hand. He stepped back as the door opened.

"David!" Sam flung her arms around his neck and hugged him. "I was just coming up to get you," she said as she ran a finger along his jaw and into the V of his shirt.

She had done a lot of thinking and remembered some advice in one of the self-help books she had read. Tonight Sam had decided she would take the lead, to make love to David her way and show him how he could make her happy.

"It took me all day to clean and set this up," Sam whispered against his neck. That was another thing she was going to have to discuss with David; he would have to help her keep the suite cleaned up. But she didn't want to let anything spoil her evening, so she tabled the annoyance until a later time. She laughed as she pulled him in, closed the door, and directed him to the exquisitely set, lace-covered table.

"I'm impressed," David said as he approached her from behind, encircled her waist, and drew her against him. Relief flooded him. All his worry had been for nothing. "Something smells wonderful."

"This . . ." Sam lifted the lid from the steaming chafing dish. "My specialty. I made it just for you . . . sautéed salmon with hollandaise."

David's heart sank to the pit of his stomach. He hated salmon, and he was allergic to eggs.

The Honeymoon Blues

Ouch! David is in trouble with a capital *T*. What will Sam do if he tells her the truth? I know what I'd do if I spent the day preparing that kind of feast! I can almost see him with yellow sauce, salmon flakes, onions, mushrooms, capers, and tomatoes running down his head and into his pockets and shoes, sitting on the deck, singing his own rendition of "The Honeymoon Blues."

We'll learn what happened to David later on. But first, I want to take a few minutes to discuss one of any relationship's greatest enemies—unrealistic expectations.

We might be tempted to laugh at David and Samantha's naïveté. Chances are, you saw some rather obvious trouble spots as they were reflecting on what they each wanted in the ideal mate. We can perhaps see what a foolish pair they are to presume so much. Sam broods because she thought David should have known instinctively how to satisfy her sexually. Later, even though she realizes the necessity for her to communicate her need, she expects that David, with a little food for thought, will change his ways.

David, on the other hand, feels responsible for Sam's happiness but is assuming that keeping their rooms clean is Sam's job. Both are still looking for the ideal, and sadly, as many couples do, may spend their entire lives trying to find it. Perhaps you are shaking your head and saying, "That's ridiculous; no one is perfect." And you are absolutely right. Yet before we criticize our fictional but all-too-real couple, perhaps we should take a moment to examine our own lives.

What Do You Expect?

You may be thinking, especially if you have already been through divorce or separation, that you've learned your lesson—you no longer expect anything from anybody. But honestly, now, is that really true? Personality Inventory 3 is a little quiz to help you determine whether or not you expect too much.

Personality Inventory 3
Unrealistic Expectations Quiz

Yes   No

Do you often find yourself disappointed:

1. ... in your mate? ☐ ☐

2. ... in friends? ☐ ☐

3. ... in a church? ☐ ☐

4. ... in your job? ☐ ☐

5. ... in yourself? ☐ ☐

6. Do you frequently find yourself wishing your circumstances could change? ☐ ☐

7. Do you feel that life should be better and that it could be if only certain people would get their act together? ☐ ☐

8. Do you often think about or use phrases like "he should," "she should," or "if only"? ☐ ☐

9. When you read Bible verses or hear particularly good points on how we are to act as Christians, do you tend to think of how they apply to others rather than how they apply to you? ☐ ☐

10. Do you ever browbeat yourself for not being good enough? ☐ ☐

If you answered yes to three or more of the questions in the quiz, chances are you are holding on to unrealistic expectations. If you do run high in the expectation department, you are certainly not alone.

As an author, speaker, and counselor, I have the opportunity to talk with many people. In listening to those people I am surprised at how many couples build their hopes for a happy marriage on a foundation of faulty expectations about both themselves and their partners.

Apparently, I'm not alone in my observations. In his book *Marital Counseling,* Norman Wright says, "There are two basic causes for trouble in a marriage: not finding in marriage what one expected to find, and not expecting what one actually finds."[1]

That was certainly true for me in my marriage; in my first years with Ron, many of my grand expectations for married life were crushed by reality's heavy hand. But I couldn't give them up because a conviction somewhere inside of me kept whispering, "Don't let facts deceive you. The ideal couple really does exist." You see, my imagination has always had the power to transform crumbled dreams—or at least to make excuses for them.

Yet if we are to eliminate a major cause of marital distress, we must somehow be willing to give up our faulty and irrational beliefs, for they are, after all, like castles made of sand— delightful to build, perhaps, but impossible to live in!

Not all expectations for marriage are troublesome, of course. I see some as valid, positive-thinking, uplifting—and necessary. We *need* hopes and dreams for ourselves and for others. But it is important to examine our expectations and not base our hopes and dreams on faulty thinking. Otherwise, we may doom ourselves and others to discouragement and failure.

In order to take a relationship beyond idealistic fantasy, it is important to: 1) understand how expectations develop; 2) distinguish between realistic and unrealistic expectations; and 3) determine the nature of our expectations.

As I share some of my experiences, you may want to jot down

your thoughts regarding unrealistic expectations you have for yourself, your partner, and your marriage. In fact, if you have a journal or have always wanted to keep one, this would be a great time to make some entries.

A Child's Perceptions

How do expectations develop? Where do our ideas about ideal relationships come from? I don't know about you, but my sand castle of expectations began when I was born. My mother had twelve brothers and sisters who thought I was adorable. I grew up in North Dakota farmland, and I remember walking through wheat fields, raking up hay in the scorching noon sun, bringing in the cows, and feasting on homemade bread, sweet cream, and fresh currant jelly. I remember playing in winter snowdrifts bigger than elephants, making snow angels, and laughing so hard I wet my pants. I remember cold winter mornings when I'd snuggle down between Mum and PaPa (my grandparents) and hug them awake. And I remember Mamma playing the guitar as we sang, "This little light of mine, I'm gonna let it shine."

Childhood had been a lovely time for me, and when I grew up I wanted my home and family to be always happy—like my "good old days." Reality gouged holes in my lovely castle one summer several years ago when I went back home for a family reunion. North Dakota was dry and dusty and flat—not at all as I'd remembered. The old farmhouse where I'd learned to walk lay crumbling under the weight of bushes and weeds. The house in town was smaller than I remembered. And alongside my glowing memories of Mum, PaPa, and Dad lurked other, darker ones—memories of sickness, worry, and fear.

As an adult I once held great and unrealistic expectations based on the mistaken belief that I had once lived an ideal life. It took a trip home—plus years of hard-core reality—to put my memories and my expectations into more realistic perspective.

I can't keep my sand-castle treasure of childhood memories—

I know that now. But maybe I'll hold on to a few grains of sand, because memories, both happy and sad, are wonderful to hold once you've made peace with the fact that you can never go back. And so I let the sand sift through my fingers and try to sing over the lump in my throat, "This little light of mine . . ." And the sand sparkles as I do, for even if my memories of an ideal childhood were faulty, the love I experienced as a child was real and precious!

"When You Wish Upon a Star"

Childhood memories gave me my first expectations of happiness. And somewhere in my youth I picked up another source of expectations—the perverse idea that if I tried hard enough, I could be perfect. I guess I'm still an optimist. Why else would I inject two star-crossed lovers, a three-hundred-foot yacht, and a guide named Kansas into the middle of a book on relationships?

Fantasies and wishes, ambitions and high hopes are like an abalone shell that glows an iridescent pink, blue, and lavender. I run my hand across the smooth mother-of-pearl texture and savor the beauty of it. But this shell comes with two sides, and if I am to own one side, I must also own the other. Shades of gray twist through the craggy drab underside to remind me that:

- for every knight in shining armor there is a horse who needs his stall cleaned.
- after every glorious weekend comes a Monday.
- failure can be as much a way of life as success.
- sorrow takes the spotlight perhaps even more often than joy.
- even though rain sometimes brings rainbows and flowers, it also brings storms that crash through lives leaving demolished homes and devastated survivors.

Even so, I think I'll keep my abalone shell of wishes and ambitions along with my sands of memory. For even though I accept that we cannot always win and that some of my expectations were too high, I still refuse to give up hope.

God Only Loves Good Girls

In dredging up my childhood beliefs, I find that I was especially influenced by faulty religious beliefs and by critical adult messages such as "Shame on you" (for making a mistake, for being naughty, for being you).

I grew up believing in God. For years, however, my idea of Christianity amounted to a fear that if I wasn't good, Jesus wouldn't like me. I thought the only way I could make heaven was to be perfect. The alternative to perfection, I'd heard, was hell.

As I pick up the shell of Christian perfection, it crumbles in my hand. I scoop the pieces into a small, clear bottle and set it next to the crumbled sand castle of childhood memories. This, too, I will keep, to remind me of how fragile I am, and how I became crushed beneath the pressures of being a perfect wife, mother, and woman of God. It will also remind me of how God scooped up a broken, shattered me and contained me in His love. He showed me that only through Christ's death and my acceptance of Him as Lord and Savior can I become flawless in His eyes.

What Are Your Expectations?

I've shared some of my expectations from childhood and adolescence that affected my adult life. How about you? Perhaps your expectations, like many of mine, emerged out of times you remember as happy. Or perhaps, like so many people I know, your expectations arose out of painful childhood memories. Regardless of the type of memory, our early years give birth to many expectations that are often shaped and colored by our fantasies. (We will further discuss the role of fantasy in the next chapter.)

Personal Inventory 4, "Uncovering Your Expectations," is designed to help you begin to unearth the source of some of your expectations and to examine whether or not those expectations are reliable. As you work through the questions, consider the way you have dealt with unrealistic expectations you have discovered in the past. Have you been able to discard them? Or did you, like me, choose to hold on to some but change the way you look at them? Are there any that you find yourself still clinging to?

Personal Inventory 4
Uncovering Your Expectations

1. What are some dreams, wishes, or fantasies from your childhood or adolescence that you've carried over into your adult life?_____

   _____

2. Take a few minutes to write down several memories that stand out in your mind._____

   _____

3. What is the overall "feel" of your childhood memories (happy, sad, painful, mixed)?_____

4. What expectations developed out of your childhood memories? You may want to list them under these categories:
   A. Expectations for self:_____

   B. Expectations for husband or wife:

   C. Expectations for marriage:_____

   D. Other expectations:_____

   _____

Once you've had the chance to explore the source of some of your expectations, I'd like to follow their often-destructive path on into adulthood. To do that, we'll need to move in closer to Reality. We'll leave the ship for a while to hike along the sea cliffs and on into the jungle to hunt for remnants of broken marriages and unfulfilled needs. But before we head into chapter 6, however, let's pause to see how David and Samantha handled the salmon incident . . .

The sun is coming up in Reality Straits. David and Samantha wake up in each other's arms, content and satiated. The fiasco of the night before turned out quite well. David had wisely thanked Sam, kissed her soundly, and told her the truth, then added, "It's the thought that counts, honey. But don't worry about the food; the only thing I'm really hungry for is you."

Chapter 6
The Seven Dragons of Expectation Caves

"YOU KNOW, SAM," David said as he pulled on his trousers, "I'm really enjoying this trip. But I can't wait to get back home. The ocean is nice to visit, and I've loved sailing ever since my navy days, but I'll take Texas any day when it comes to settling down."

Sam tucked the pillows neatly under the bedspread and straightened. "You're from Texas? I thought you were from Los Angeles."

"What gave you that idea? Sure, I keep an apartment in L.A. because my architectural firm is there. But my home base is and always has been in Texas. I need wide-open spaces. There's nothing like a campfire out under the stars and wind lulling you to sleep at roundup time. I know you'll feel the same way, Sam—once you get settled . . ."

Sam stiffened. Roundups? Campfires? This was not the same David she married. Her David was an architect, a man who liked ballet and dining out in restaurants on top of tall buildings. "I don't understand, David. Are you saying you want us to *live* in Texas?"

"Well, of course. Where else?" David drew Sam into the circle of his arms, but she backed away.

"I thought we were going to live in Malibu."

"Malibu?" David laughed, his tone mocking. "California is no place to raise kids. Besides, I'm selling my firm in L.A."

Sam pointed her finger at him and poked him in the chest. "What do you mean you can't raise kids in California? I was raised there—are you saying there's something wrong with me?"

"Of course not, honey," he said as he lifted his hands defensively and backed toward the door. This was not going the way he'd planned. "Look, let's calm down and discuss this thing like two adults. I know living on a ranch will take some getting used to, but it's a good, clean, wholesome life. I've always dreamed of getting married and settling down there. Can't you just see us sitting on the old porch swing, watching the daylight settle behind Sunset Rocks? You looking prettier than the day we married, holding our new baby boy to your breast. And me, telling you how much I love you."

"No! If you expect me to live in Texas, you're crazy." She may have married David for better or worse, but she did not marry him for Texas! "How do you expect me to live in a desert surrounded by cactus and tumbleweeds? I'd dry up. And what about my job? Why can't we sit in *my* swing and watch the sun go down in the Pacific Ocean?"

Worry furrowed David's brow. "Sam, I can't believe we're arguing about this. Texas is not all desert, and we won't be all that far from the city. A man's wife goes where his work takes him. And mine happens to be running a horse ranch in Texas. You'll just have to cut back on your work. Maybe you can telecommute or something. But I make enough to support us. And if you're worried about keeping up the house, I've got that covered." David smiled, thinking he'd found a solution to their dilemma. "My mother and grandmother have agreed to stay on."

"Your what?" Sam bellowed. "David, you sound like something out of an old John Wayne movie. I know your type—keep 'em barefoot and pregnant and down on the farm, then throw in good old Mom to make sure the little woman behaves herself. Oh, no! The only way you'll get me to Texas, David Hartley, is in a pine box!" Sam picked up a shoe and threw it at David's head. He ducked and it hit the door.

With a stubborn set to his jaw David declared, "I'll get you to that ranch if I have to hogtie you and carry you there." He walked out, slamming the door behind him.

Unrealistic Expectations

Ouch! It looks like the honeymoon is definitely over for Sam and David. Let's just hope we aren't witnessing the end of their marriage as well. Fortunately, Reality Straits and Reconciliation Bay hold some solutions for them if they are willing to adjust.

David and Sam have several unrealistic expectations, some of which we discovered in the last chapter. Now we see that:

- David expects her to follow him anywhere.
- He expects her to love Texas because he does.
- Sam expects to keep her job, live in Malibu, and stay married to David, who wants to live in Texas.
- David expects Sam to agree to live with his mother and grandmother.

We could go on, but you get the idea. You may be wondering why Sam and David are having such a hard time communicating. Perhaps their lack of communication is leading to unrealistic expectations, or quite possibly the expectations are leading to poor communication. Whatever the cause, if they want their relationship to work, they'd better start talking. Of course there are effective and noneffective methods of communication, and we'll be dealing with those in chapter 13. But for now, let's go out on deck and see what the day holds.

The first part of our visit to Reality will include a trip through Expectation Caves. This is where we'll examine more deeply the unrealistic expectations we have for ourselves, for others, and for marriage. We'll see how these expectations can house some very destructive elements and then learn some constructive ways to deal with our expectations.

An Adventure in Reality

As you can probably tell by the title of this chapter, we're headed for our first real adventure. We survived a long, stormy night, but blue skies promise a lovely day for an excursion up to Anticipation Bluff. David eases the boat into the narrow waterway of Reality Straits. Steep sea cliffs rise off a rocky beach on both sides of the yacht, then level off to a grassy meadow littered with wildflowers. Buoys mark the water's depth, and David carefully navigates within the safety zone. The crew drops anchor in a sheltered cove, and our adventure begins.

To add color and a bit of excitement to the day, Kansas has taken on the role of a crusty *Treasure Island* pirate. Dressed in a red-and-white striped shirt, with black curly wig, a false beard, and a black patch over one eye, he positions himself in the eight-person lifeboat. "All ashore that's goin' ashore!" he calls in a salty, seafaring brogue. His theatrics remind me that reality can be both fun and adventurous.

We clamber overboard and drop into the waiting rowboat. Equipped with a treasure map, hiking boots, ropes, and food for thought, we're off to explore Expectation Caves.

Once on shore, we waste no time scaling the jagged rocks, inspired by what we expect to find in the dark and mysterious caverns spotting the sea walls.

"As legend would have it," Kansas drawls in his raspy pirate's voice, "the caves hold a treasure more valuable than silver or gold. It's rumored that they hold the key to everlasting happiness. But, mates," he adds, "in order to find the key, ye must first conquer the dragons who guard the inner chambers."

I shudder, having personally come head to head with the lot of them. The dragons he's referring to are those created out of our unfulfilled expectations and fantasies. We'll be confronting those dragons in a few minutes. But before we get too far along in our story, perhaps I should clarify a thing or two about fantasies.

The Benefits of Fantasy

In the first place, fantasies aren't necessarily bad or dangerous. In fact, many psychologists tell us they can be a helpful tool for dealing with stress or emotional problems or for fulfilling unmet needs. As Lucy Freeman says in her book *What Do Women Want?* "In providing a momentary escape from real life, fantasy helps us endure it with more grace, dignity, and humor than we might otherwise muster. Fantasy gives us a sense of independence. . . . We depend only on our imagination to fulfill our wishes. . . . Everyone can concoct the most exotic and erotic love scenes, or the bloodiest of revenges."[1]

For children, especially, fantasy can serve as a friend that distorts reality enough so that they can conquer "monsters" that are otherwise too big for them to handle—abuse, neglect, or even the too-high expectations of those who love them. Many of our current expectations grew out of fantasies we developed in the past to help us feel secure and competent and loved.

But fantasies, whether born in children or adults, are not just therapeutic; they can be a source of harmless fun.

I realize there are people who would argue with me about the benefits of fantasy, saying that, especially for adults, they are a frivolous waste of time. Skeptics might say, "You should take life more seriously" or "You should be devoting your time to studying the Bible and working toward a higher level of holiness."

But I would argue that God gave us a beautiful gift of imagination that can help us work out problems, develop goals, see visions, dream dreams, and offer hope. Perhaps most wonderful of all, it is a means through which God communicates with us.

So, as I speak negatively about fantasies and expectations in the next few pages, bear in mind I'm talking about *unrealistic expectations* and *fantasies that distort reality*. These are the breed of fantasies that can become a hazard to our mental and emotional health.

Seven Deadly Dragons

Do you remember "Puff the Magic Dragon," a popular song in the sixties? Puff was a mystical dragon who lived in an imaginary cave by the sea. Puff frolicked with Jackie, the little boy who'd dreamed him into being. But as Jackie grew older, he left Puff and other childish things behind.

When we grow up, we store our toys in the attic and relinquish our mystical, magical childhood to some remote, cobwebbed corner of our minds. But not always—as we saw in the last chapter. Sometimes fantasies grow out of our childhood experiences and spill into adulthood, distorting our images of what we can realistically expect from one another.

Romantic notions, high hopes, lofty ideals, and dreams of a good life in never-never land, when taken to the extreme, can lead us down the rocky trail toward dragons of another, more evil nature. They float obscurely in the mist surrounding reality, hiding in expectation's empty caverns. They infiltrate our relationships and undermine our efforts for peace and commitment. If unchecked, they may deliver married people into the misery of divorce.

Unrealistic fantasies can start as innocently as a cute little dragon named Puff. But they can grow into destructive forces from which we cannot escape—not even in our dreams.

Aspirations of a New Bride

Are you fighting with dragons lurking in expectations that didn't come true? Have unrealistic expectations affected your relationships? Have they clouded your ability to think clearly?

They did mine. In my youth, unrealistic expectations blinded me to the nitty-gritty reality of simply *coexisting* with another human.

At nineteen, I met Ron and fell in love. I guess part of the reason I wrote a trip through the Fantasy Islands into this book and introduced characters like Samantha and David is that in those early days of our courtship, I was oblivious to the possible problems that could develop in a relationship. My prince had come along to sweep me off my feet.

My world became the fantasy I'd always dreamed it would be as I involved myself in the very romantic and fairy-tale-like task of creating a beautiful wedding and a satin gown fit for a princess. Like many couples, our first six months revolved around falling in love, pleasing each other, making a good impression, getting married, and riding off happily into the sunset.

No wonder, after the honeymoon, so many of us wake up next to the stranger we married and say, "Oh, Lord . . . what have I done?"

I've heard it said that God gave us infatuation and romance to blind us to the hardships in relationships because if people knew what living together was really like, they'd probably never marry, mate, multiply, and subdue the earth.

But does God cause temporary blindness? I doubt it. That wouldn't be in character with the God who, in the person of Jesus, said, "Then you will know the truth, and the truth will set you free" (John 8:32 NIV).

I think God would want us to know the truth and to plan ahead. Didn't He indicate that when He said, "For which one of you, when he wants to build a tower, does not first sit down and calculate the cost, to see if he has enough to complete it? Otherwise, when he has laid a foundation, and is not able to finish, all who observe it begin to ridicule him" (Luke 14:28–29).

Finally, I imagine God would like us to ask His direction: "A man's mind plans his way, but the Lord directs his steps" (Proverbs 16:9 RSV).

Getting to Know You

I think most of us would agree that young couples should get to know each other well before committing to marriage. (I personally think two years would be good.) Unfortunately, in this age of instant potatoes, cameras, and love affairs, *wait* is becoming a four-letter word. And most couples spend their time getting acquainted with all the "beautiful and new" details of each other and all too often overlook the potential problems.

For example, my fiancé never gazed deeply into my eyes and whispered, "Darling, I leave the cap off the toothpaste and, what's worse, I squeeze it in the middle."

He never dropped to his knees to say, "You'd make me the happiest man in the world if you'd marry me . . . oh, and by the way, when I watch sports of any kind, don't bother talking to me because I won't listen."

And I never told him I strongly believed mothers with small children should not work outside the home. What I said was, "Honey, I'll be happy to work while you finish college."

I certainly didn't tell him that the real reason I wanted to marry him was to have the security of a healthy, strong, and permanent father. (My father had been ill off and on during my childhood, and I later came to realize that I, through no fault of my father's, had often felt abandoned.)

Maybe I didn't say those things because I didn't know what I was feeling. At nineteen I barely knew who I was. Besides, what red-blooded girl whose hormones are telling her it's time to get married and have babies is going to come up for air after a five-minute kiss and say, "I have a confession to make. You see,

I'm entrapped in a dysfunctional family system and, rather than looking for a husband, I'm actually seeking a father figure because I haven't resolved the oedipal complex of my childhood.

"And to top it all off, in order to recalibrate my dysfunctional family system into a homeostatic state, I became a parentified child (which, of course, means I took on my missing parent's role), and as such will probably cause conflict in our relationship."

To which my befuddled boyfriend would probably have replied, "W-what? . . ."

Premarital Counseling Can Help

Unfortunately, most couples in love don't deal with the nitty-gritty details and potential problems of life. It just isn't romantic! But neither, of course, are disillusionment, separation, and divorce! Even though I made fun of the business of getting to know your potential marriage partner, I'm a strong advocate of premarital counseling. And I don't mean the kind of counseling Ron and I went through, which consisted of spending a few hours with a pastor talking about important data such as who's going to give the bride away. I'm talking about in-depth discussion on the realities of living together. Six weeks of learning about family backgrounds, personality traits, areas of conflict (such as finances, friends, and rearing children), and discovering effective ways to communicate gives the couple a reality-based foundation.

Concrete statistics aren't available as yet, but many counselors report that couples who go through premarital counseling have a better chance of staying married because counseling helps couples understand what marital problems might develop and teaches them how to deal with those problems. Counselors also report that many of the young people they counsel end up not getting married. Not a happy ending, true, but isn't it better to find out you're not made for each other before, rather than after, the wedding?

Much of the time, of course, the couple is too preoccupied with romance to benefit from even the best premarital counseling. Bruce Larson, in his book *Faith for the Journey*, suggests a possible alternative:

> As a pastor I do a good deal of marriage counseling. I often wish that I could delay that counseling until three months after the wedding. It's hard to suggest to a couple, starry-eyed and infatuated with each other, that there will be problems and pitfalls ahead. They just don't believe it. I think they'd be better equipped some three months into the marriage to understand some of the things I'm talking about.[2]

But whether it happens before or after the wedding, a couple considering marriage can benefit from an accurate assessment of what marriage will be like after the honeymoon. Had Ron and I known then what we know now . . .

Give Me Stability, Security, and Predictability (Plus Romance), and I'll Follow You Anywhere

Besides romance and happiness ever after, Ron and I wanted what most couples want in a marriage—stability, security, and predictability. On the surface, those wants may sound quite reasonable, but are they? Christian psychologist Norman Wright suggests another way of looking at these three seemingly harmless desires:

- *Stability* . . . resistance to change. Stability is a property that restores a disturbed substance to its original state; it restores equilibrium. Most of us don't like change and tend to resist it.

106

- *Security* . . . having all of our needs fulfilled by this one person we plan to spend forever with.
- *Predictability* . . . knowing what to expect. "Having the ability to predict the future, at least in general ways, gives us a feeling of control."[3]

As happens in so many marriages, Ron and I had needs that couldn't be fulfilled, partly because we each wanted someone to provide what was missing in our own lives, and partly because no human being can prevent change, meet every need, or control the future. Which brings us back to the dragons . . .

My Life With the Dragons

Ron and I have a lot in common—we're both human, and we're both consistently stubborn. I'm an artist. He thinks art is nice but doesn't provide much job security. He enjoys sports. I enjoy shopping while he watches sports. He prefers orderliness and getting one job done before he starts another. I'd like to be orderly, but it's hard when you have four hundred unfinished projects scattered all over the house.

We have a few differences, too. I love to cook gourmet meals. He doesn't like to eat experiments. Over the course of our life together, we approached raising kids, managing money, and family life as though we'd been brought up in two different homes . . . which, of course, we were. I'd tell you more, but by now I'm sure you get the picture. We are two people who have lived life in different ways, each hoping the other would eventually come to see the light.

Twenty years ago Ron and I climbed the rocky cliffs of Reality's shoreline together, discovering to our dismay that Expectation Caves were infested with seven bad-tempered dragons: Disappointment, Disillusionment, Discouragement, Discontentment, Dissatisfaction, Despondency, and Despair.

In the early part of our marriage, I pretended the seven dragons were only figments of my imagination. Remember, I grew up thinking that, ideally, Christians didn't give way to unpleasant thoughts, and certainly, joyful people couldn't experience despair. And songs and storybooks had assured me that everything would turn out all right. I struggled to maintain the façade of being the perfect wife, mother, nurse, and all-around woman of the year. When one ideal image crumbled, I simply pulled myself together and created another.

I was an idealist who expected that somehow I could patch up the world and in the process find the happiness that seemed to fill everyone's life but mine.

Discontentment, Disappointment, and Disillusionment reared their ugly heads. Daily they grew more persistent, breaking out in fits of anger, frustration, and misery. But I was made of sturdy stock, raised to keep my emotions under control.

Besides, I lived in the era of the Supermoms, and super mothers didn't give up; they just flew faster. Perfectionists are not easily subdued. I worked outside my home. I kept my home nearly spotless, sewed for the kids and me, volunteered as a health-room mother, dutifully attended PTA meetings, created gourmet meals, spent "quality" time with my kids, worked to be a supportive wife and creative lover to my husband.

Then one day, while trying to go faster than a speeding bullet, I crash-landed off the rocky coast of Reality. Despondency tore me apart and threw me in a pit of gloom, bitterness, sorrow, and emptiness . . . a dark tomb from which I could see no escape.

Discouragement and Discontentment hovered over me, blocking all means of escape, yelling obscenities like, "You should have known better," "It's all your fault," and "If only you hadn't gotten married . . . had kids . . . been born."

Disillusionment stomped black inky footprints all over my images of Mary Poppins, Pollyanna, and the virtuous woman in Proverbs.

Disappointment showed me that no one had lived up to my expectations of them. Dissatisfaction told me I was a fool for caring about others and urged me to spend more time worrying about myself.

Despondency said I had no worth.

But the hardest of all to face was Despair, who constantly took it upon herself to remind me that I'd failed myself—and worse, I had failed God.

I called to the Lord to rescue me, but I heard nothing but the echo of my bitter cries for help. The seven dragons had conquered me. And as if to prolong my misery, they led me directly into chambers of the most destructive dragons of all, Depression and Death. And I began to wonder if the world might not be better off without me.

A Challenge to Change

Unrealistic expectations can destroy a life; they nearly did mine. If you're a person who holds fast to idealistic expectations for yourself, for others, or for marriage, you'll probably face the dragons, too, if you haven't already.

How do we escape the dragons' lairs of unrealistic expectations? In his book *The Pillars of Marriage*, Norman Wright says, "Each individual enters marriage with both an overt and a hidden set of expectations for the marriage and the partner's behavior and performance. . . . When these expectations are all brought into the open, evaluated, challenged and discussed, greater harmony comes to the marriage."[4]

If we have high expectations of ourselves and of others, we will do well to remember that God does not expect us to be more than what He created us to be. What right have we, then, to expect anyone to meet our criteria for the way we think they should be? In her book *What Is a Family?* Edith Schaeffer writes, "When people insist on perfection or nothing, they get nothing. . . . The waste of what *could* be, by demanding what *cannot* be, is something we all have lived through in certain periods of our lives, but which we need to put behind us with resolve."[5]

Good advice. If you didn't do so in the last chapter, you may want to make a list of your expectations. Writing down our thoughts helps bring them into the open.

Now comes the evaluation part. Consider the validity of each expectation on your list. Do they call for someone to change so that he or she will better fit your model? Be wary of expectations that begin with: "I should," "he or she should," and "we should."

By now you probably have a good idea of what is realistic and what isn't. If not, discuss your expectations with a friend. Cross out those on your list that you've determined are unrealistic. For example, I had to cross out, "Ron should give up watching television sports."

You may feel that some of your expectations are valid. For example, "I expect my husband/wife to be faithful," or "My wife should stop hitting me with her rolling pin" are valid points and lie in the realm of possibility. You may have some entirely realistic items on your list that call for you or your partner to make some vital changes. Leave them.

When you've finished, tuck your list away until chapter 7, where we'll talk about what happens when realistic expectations are not met. Now, however, I'd like a chance to show you how I, with a little help from a Friend, managed to slay the seven dragons of Expectation Caves.

A Dragon on My Back

Not everyone has to end up with a dragon on his or her back to realize that human beings are not now, nor have they been since the Fall, perfect. And I don't think everyone clings as stubbornly as I did to the desire for perfection. It took an acute attack of depression to make me see how black a hole unrealistic expectations can become.

Depression stripped me of my dignity and pride. At first I cried, "God, how could You let this happen to me? Christians shouldn't get depressed." Finally, because I had nothing left, I gave up and whimpered, "God, help me."

In the silent night the turmoil ended. A Presence far greater than I had slain the dragons that had tormented me. A sense of calm enveloped me, and the cave which entombed me was transformed into a warm, comforting womb through which God nurtured me. And as the psalmist wrote: "I waited patiently for God to help me; then he listened and heard my cry. He lifted me out of the pit of despair, out from the bog and the mire, and set my feet on a hard, firm path and steadied me as I walked along. He has given me a new song . . ." (Psalms 40:1–3 TLB).

I spent time in counseling, learning the truth about faulty expectations. And I spent time with God, who showed me how to delight in His creation . . . how to love . . . how to think true, honorable, right, pure, and lovely thoughts—realistic thoughts about myself as well as others. He showed me that when I learn to see the world through His eyes I can accept people—even myself, my husband, and my marriage—as they are. I discovered the hidden treasure that lies beyond the expectations is the cross of Jesus Christ—the key to salvation.

The womb opened. God rebirthed me into a new life. And I couldn't wait to tell others what God had done. As I stepped out of Expectation Caves, a warm sun greeted me and took away the chill. A gentle sea breeze caressed my skin. I admired the earth God had created and the place He had given me in it. I looked at my husband, my children, myself, and saw that we were not perfect but good—and very, very real.

The bright gold sun is dissolving into the western sea as we, too, emerge from Expectation Caves. Rose and lavender trim the puffy clouds on the horizon. Tired from a full day of discovery, we climb aboard the lifeboat and head for the yacht anchored offshore. Reality, we've found, holds many secrets and exposes many dreams. Within her borders we find pain and suffering. Yet she holds a beauty that transcends any cross we'll ever have to bear, for God's holy Presence permeates reality and gives us hope.

It's time to say good-bye to Expectation Caves and their draconic inhabitants as we move on to chapter 7, where we'll check in on David and Samantha as they wonder, *Can this marriage be saved?* Then we'll watch firsthand as the rocks of Reality tear asunder other marital myths and legends we have known.

Chapter 7
How to Change the
One You Love

"WHERE DID I go wrong?" Samantha asked herself as she paced the floor of the stateroom she had shared with David. "I thought we were an ideal match. How could something that seemed so right turn out so wrong? How can he expect me to change my whole life to suit him?"

Sam, a voice in her head seemed to say, *aren't you expecting him to change for you?* Sam frowned. "Yes," she answered herself, "but I'm not asking him to give up everything he's worked for and move to Texas."

It seemed so hopeless. Maybe it would be best if they went their separate ways—now, before there were any children. They'd reached an impasse, and there was no way Sam could back down. She had seen her mother give in to her father's demands time and again. "I will not be backed into a corner like a scared rabbit," she said aloud as if to confirm her convictions.

Reluctantly Sam made her way to the upper deck to tell David of her decision. He would probably be happy to see her go. He apparently wanted a docile, submissive woman who'd let him walk all over her. Well, he'd have to look elsewhere.

Sam stopped abruptly when she saw David. He was leaning against the railing, and his pensive, unhappy expression abated Sam's anger. Desire, compassion, and love welled up inside her, and for a moment Sam felt a strong urge to run into David's arms and tell him she would move to the moon with him if it would make him happy. But she didn't. Too many questions stood in the way. If David really loved her, he'd live in Malibu . . . wouldn't he? Sam was sure that if he'd just try it for a while, she could change his mind. This, after all, was the twentieth century; men should be able to move where a woman's job takes her.

David gazed into the crystal-blue water and watched it lap lazily against the ship's bow. He had been thinking long and hard over their argument earlier that morning and had even considered going home without her.

But he loved Samantha. He couldn't believe he'd actually threatened to tie her up and haul her off to Texas. He wouldn't, of course, though the idea sorely tempted him. If living in Texas meant losing Sam . . . he didn't want to think about that.

David shook his head and sighed. Somehow it just didn't seem right to give up your dreams just to make a woman happy. If Sam really loved him, she would go anywhere with him. Maybe he could persuade her to visit the ranch for a couple of months. He knew he could turn her into a rancher if he just had a little more time.

David turned from the rail and saw Sam. As she moved toward him his heart pounded in his chest as though he'd just run a race. He'd give up a dozen ranches for Sam, but he had to know if she loved him enough to make that sacrifice.

"Hi," she said in a breathless whisper.

"Sam, I owe you an apology for this morning." David took her hand in his. "I guess we should have talked about where we were going to live before we got married."

"I guess we should have."

"I don't want to lose you, Sam."

"I know . . . but I can't move to Texas with you, David. I can't give up all I've worked for . . . my office, my home. . . . My roots are here . . ."

She didn't love him. David struggled for control. He was a man, and men didn't cry. "I guess . . ." he hesitated, battling to talk around the lump in his throat ". . . this is good-bye, then."

He waited a moment for Sam's reply, but none came. Sam watched David walk away, wanting to run after him. Yet she stood firm, cemented to her principles. A dull, throbbing ache began in her chest and radiated through every part of her body. Finally, unable to stand any longer, she sank to her knees and gave herself up to the sobs that shook her body. She had kept her identity—had preserved her freedom to live in Malibu and keep her penthouse office. And all it had cost her was the only man she had ever loved.

Paradise Lost

Will David and Samantha really give up a chance to live together as a couple committed to each other in marriage? Should Sam give up her career? Her home? Should David give up his ranch? Is there any hope that either of them will change?

Many of our marital spats are based on preconceived ideas about what married life should be like and what roles we should play. Akin to unrealistic expectations are the many myths that we come to accept as fact, when in truth they are only illusions that hinder us from seeing men, women, and marriage as they really are, in an attitude of nonjudgment. Maybe we'll find some answers in Reconciliation Bay. But in the meantime, let's get on with our tour.

The Temple of Doomed Relationships

Today in Reality Straits we'll be traveling inland through the jungle to examine the remains of the Temple of Doomed Relationships. In the next few chapters we'll seek to uncover searing evidence as to whether or not:

- you can change the one you love.
- romantic novels, sexual fantasies, and pornography enhance a relationship.
- divorce is the answer to incompatibility.
- two halves really do make a whole.

Kansas joins us, decked out once again in his jungle attire. "I'm doing a documentary on the Temple of Doomed Relationships, and I've chartered a tour boat to take us up the river. The temple lies in the heart of Reality's jungle. Not too many signed up for this trip, I'm sorry to say. Some said they'd rather not learn the truth about what they believe, because it's too hard to change, and truth might make them feel guilty.

"They'll be sorry they didn't come," Kansas continues, "because truth offers freedom once you're able to grasp it."

There is a wistfulness in Kansas I haven't seen before, and I wonder briefly about the significance of this trip for him. But as quickly as the melancholy came, it is gone.

"To get to the temple," he says in an animated tone, "we'll travel inland up the river that leads into the heart of Reality. You'll want to watch for pythons, low-hanging vines, and crocodiles." He laughs and adds, "Ah, there's a croc now."

As I gaze along the river's edge, seeing only dead logs and lush tropical plants, Kansas dips his oar in the water and sends a water shower onto a muddy bank. The log I've been staring at springs into action, flips his tail, and splashes angrily into the water. He vanishes—all fifteen feet of him. My heart thuds. I stare into the menacing black water, half expecting him to flip the boat and eat us for dinner.

As Kansas expertly guides the boat deeper into the primitive rain forest, I marvel at the jungle's eerie green depths, home to millions of species of plants and animals. I remember news items I've heard lately about how farmers and developers are destroying millions of acres of rain forest for wood, farming, cattle ranches, dams, and roads.

What a tragedy, I muse. *God gave human beings dominion over the earth to protect the people and the animals, but some people, in their greed for temporary money and power, are destroying it.*

I don't want the jungle to change. Instead, I want to alter the minds and hearts of the people bent on ravaging the earth.

But people are not easily changed.

He'll Never Change

The subject of change is an interesting one. If you want to get a few laughs in a group of older women, all you have to say is, "I thought my husband would change." Sadly, the laughter has a hard edge to it. But then I guess there's nothing truly funny about a relationship in which one partner is always after the other to mend his or her ways.

I have a good friend, Jeannette, whose husband is an alcoholic. Phil doesn't drink often, but when he does, he becomes violent. Phil has also been involved with other women. "I've lost count of the number of times I've forgiven him and let him come back home. The last time, he agreed to counseling, and I really thought we'd be okay, then he started drinking and womanizing again. He's gone now, and I don't know if I'll ever take him back. I love him, but he has to change."

You Can't Change People

Intellectually, we know that it is practically impossible to change people. We also know there are no perfect people, and that when we become involved in a relationship, we must compromise some of our wants and needs. Yet knowing this doesn't seem to stop our insatiable appetite for trying to make people over.

I suppose it has something to do with some deep dream within us to scourge the world of ugliness, dirty politics, nuclear weapons, racism, hunger, and war. Or perhaps, even more, our wanting people to change springs from our selfish desire to always have things our own way. Still, one can only wonder if this driving need for change doesn't partially reflect the desperate need within us to return to the perfect image in which God originally created us.

The Psychiatrist and the Light Bulb

I turn my thoughts back to the jungle and the tour boat that is taking us deeper into the dense tropical forest. "What's the answer?" I ask Kansas. "There are so many people who could be so much happier if they would only change."

"Your talking about change reminds me of a joke," he says.

I'm not in the mood for jokes, but I decide to humor him.

"How many psychiatrists does it take to change a light bulb?" Kansas asks.

"Six," I answer smugly. "One to hold the bulb and five to turn the ladder around."

"Wrong. Only one, but the light bulb has to really *want* to change."

Once again Kansas has, as the old cliché goes, "hit the nail on the head." Being involved in counseling, I know that no matter how much you do or say, a person will only really reform if he or she wants to. Even then, the task can at times seem insurmountable. As another old saying goes, "You can lead a horse to water, but you can't make him drink."

One example might be the man who comes into the counselor's office and says in a surly tone, "My wife said I had to come in and get counseling or she'd divorce me. She says I have a problem with my temper . . . so fix it." No counselor can "fix" a person, especially one who looks like he could sub for Rambo and would rather rearrange your face than let you suggest how he might alter his lifestyle.

To complicate matters, Rambo has not admitted to having a problem. His wife *says* he has a problem. Eventually, if he is put under enough pressure to either alter his disposition or find himself out on the street, he may make some changes. But Rambo is not making these changes for himself. And within a couple of months the façade cracks and the rage returns, perhaps with even more force, because now it's accompanied by fear that his wife may follow through with the divorce. Guilt stalks him, but instead of owning up to his faults, he blames others.

Am I saying that bringing about change in people is a hopeless task? No. I don't think any person or situation is beyond hope. I often hear true stories of people who have recovered from addictions and from destructive lifestyles. What I am saying is that in order for a person to change, that person must 1) have the knowledge that he or she is behaving in a detrimental way and 2) be motivated to change. And there's always the possibility that if you keep the horse at the water trough long enough he might get thirsty.

If Your Partner Needs to Change

If your spouse or someone else close to you needs to change, here are some steps you might want to take:

1. *Determine what changes you see as necessary.* Write down how and why you'd like the other person to change. Ask him or her to make a similar list about you. (It may hurt, but it's only fair.)

2. *Now write down all the things you like about each other.* Include fond memories and good times from the past. What attracted you to him or her?

3. *Consider the following questions:*

· Is the relationship worth saving? Why?
· Do you love the other person?

- Do you consider him or her a friend?
- Do you stay in the relationship out of fear? need? (I'll be talking about addictive relationships later.)
- If the other person is your spouse, would you marry him or her again?

4. *Now lay down your pen and pad and with your eyes closed, envision the other person as the victim of a tragic accident or disease that takes him or her away from you.* Think about what life would be like without that person. If he or she is your spouse, what would it be like to live in your home, sleep, eat without him or her? While you may find the task unpleasant, there is an advantage to knowing what you'll miss before it's gone.

Cal, a man of fifty-two, who lost his wife of twenty-eight years to cancer, said, "Sometimes, I used to think about how uncomplicated my life would be without Susan to nag me about things. Now I'd give anything to hear her telling me to pick up the newspapers, take out the trash, or put my shoes in the bedroom where they belong. We did everything together, my Susan and me. I honestly don't know how I'm going to get along without her."

5. *Evaluate how serious the problem really is.* Naturally, as we think of changes we'd like to make, some of them may be exasperating irritations that we've grown tired of putting up with. There have been times in my relationship with Ron that I have thought, *I swear if he tells that story again I'm leaving.* But when I want to change something about my husband, I must first consider my own attitudes. Have unrealistic expectations crept into my desires for change? Do I want to turn him into something he's not? Am I still trying to change the man to fit my image of what marriage should be?

In some cases, however, change may be vital to emotional and even physical health. One woman, Peggy, said, "My doctor told me that if I didn't get out of my situation, I would die. The stress and emotional abuse I was getting from my husband was literally killing me."

Counseling and eventual change is a must for healing relationships caught up in emotional or physical abuse, drug or alcohol addiction (and other harmful addictive behaviors), violence, and unfaithfulness.

6. *Take your list of changes and examine them again.* With each item, ask these questions: If obtaining this change means losing the other person, would I still insist on it? Is this behavior emotionally, physically, and spiritually detrimental to myself? My family?

7. *Consider your options.* If you conclude the change is necessary, you have several options:

- You can say and do nothing and continue to be miserable.
- You can leave the other person.
- You can tell the other person that either he or she changes his or her ways or you want out of the relationship.
- You can negotiate by respectfully confronting the other person with your concerns.
- You can see a counselor.
- You can see a lawyer.
- You can facilitate change by making changes in yourself. (This last option may be especially important.)

There are cases where some or all of these steps may be appropriate. But once again, people can change only if they really want to. Manipulation, force, criticism, or honest confrontation may start the changing process, but we all know that no matter what happens to us, we each are equipped with a will and the freedom to choose our own way.

Seek God's Direction

As we seek necessary changes and alter our own attitudes about what's really important in our lives, an essential part of our plans must be seeking God's direction through prayer and fellowship with God and with others. The Lord can alter circumstances and heal broken hearts. He can give us the strength, unconditional love, and grace we need to confront in a respectful and caring way.

God doesn't want our relationships to end. But He certainly doesn't want greed, selfishness, broken promises, addictive substances, and violence to destroy His beloved children.

We've traveled ten miles into the jungle by now. The thick forest walls have thinned out and we can see open fields where animals graze. "Oh, this is wonderful," I say, relieved at the change in the landscape. "I feel light and free. Funny, I hadn't noticed it until now, but with the density of the plant life closing in on us from the riverbanks . . . I felt, I don't know, claustrophobic, I guess."

"A lot of people feel that way," Kansas says. "It's amazing how a change in scenery makes people act and feel different."

"Yes, yes it is," I muse.

"And you're thinking that's the way it is with people. Often, when you change, you also bring about change in the people around you."

"You sound like someone with experience," I observe. "Have you made some changes in your life?"

Kansas turns away from my gaze, but not before I catch a glimpse of the sorrow I saw earlier. "Yes," he says as he fixes his gaze on some spot on the far horizon. "But my changes came too late."

I don't pursue it. Maybe he'll share the source of his grief a little later. What he said about changing ourselves gives me more than enough to think about now.

Changing Ourselves

Too often we seek to change others when we should be working on altering our own lives and attitudes. It's easy to forget

Jesus' sharp reprimand in Matthew 7:1–5, where He tells us that if we judge others we will be judged the same way. He also said, "Why do you look at the speck of sawdust in your brother's eye and pay no attention to the plank in your own eye? . . . You hypocrite, first take the plank out of your own eye, and then you will see clearly to remove the speck from your brother's eye" (vv. 3, 5 NIV).

The man whose wife is an alcoholic must remove the plank from his eye so that he can see his situation clearly. By lying and making excuses for her, he is not protecting his family. Rather, he is encouraging his wife to continue drinking. He must change. He must say, "No more."

Similarly, every woman who continues to live with an abusive husband is guilty of enabling him to abuse her. To alter the relationship it is she, not he, who must take the initial step. She must step out of her victim role and say, "No! No more." If the situation is to be remedied, she must facilitate the change.

The Problem With Submission

Some of you may be furrowing your brow and saying, "But what about those Bible verses that tell us wives are to be submissive to their husbands?"

Jennifer endured years of abuse because she thought wives should be submissive regardless of what a husband is or does. She believed that she was making her husband angry, and that somehow, if she stayed in submission and servitude, trying to please him, she'd win his approval and he wouldn't have to hurt her anymore.

That is so wrong. True, the Bible tells women to submit or be subject to and obey their husbands, but too often people don't understand what that really means. To be subject does not mean being subservient, second-class, inferior, and nonassertive. Instead it means freely giving loyalty and allegiance to a mate. Subjecting to a man means being faithful, obliging, willing, flexible, and adaptable. It means blending with, consenting to. To subject oneself to another is to entrust yourself to that person's care.

Submission does not give a man the right to violate his wife or disregard other scriptural principles.

Many difficulties arise in husband/wife roles because men and women get stuck on one verse and don't read the rest of God's directions.

Men, too, are called to submit to their wives. In fact, just before the verse that reads, "Wives, submit to your husbands . . ." comes the one that says, "Submit to one another out of reverence for Christ" (Ephesians 5:21 NIV).

And then, after giving wives a brief message on submission, the apostle Paul lays a heavy load of responsibility on men:

> For the husband is the head of the wife as Christ is the head of the church, his body, of which he is the Savior. . . . Husbands, love your wives, just as Christ loved the church and gave himself up for her to make her holy, cleansing her by the washing with water through the word, and to present her to himself as a radiant church, without stain or wrinkle or any other blemish, but holy and blameless (Ephesians 5:23, 25 NIV).

I see no mention here of slapping a wife around to get her to bow to a man's demands. Or criticizing, belittling, blaming; or beating her into submission by lashing out with words that leave deep, debilitating wounds. What I see is a picture of a man who loves his wife so much that he would sacrifice his life for hers. I see a man who would take her pain and suffering upon himself. I see a man who is courageous, a shepherd, a nurturer—a leader who sees the beauty of God's creation and the gifts and talents that are uniquely his wife's and seeks to let her shine. I see a man who is content to let her light glorify him.

I suggest that any man who would treat his wife as Christ treated His church would have little trouble gaining the respect, submission, and love he desires and that God had originally planned from the woman he marries. We would all do well to study what God says about marriage and about the roles husbands and wives are to play.

Men Are Abused, Too

I realize I've been pretty tough on the men in this section. And I'll be the first to agree that men perhaps as often as women come through marriage carrying scars from emotional and—less often—physical abuse. I've seen men torn apart by uncaring, selfish women who took advantage of their generosity, gentleness, and respect.

There are too many women and men who endeavor to be loving, caring, submissive people and who all too often are walked on, taken advantage of, and mistreated. Sadly, we will always encounter vain and greedy people, both men and women, who take advantage of what they see as weakness. We will do well to love one another enough to learn when and how to confront—and, if necessary, have the courage to walk away.

Tough Love—the Biblical Approach

Some of you may be saying, "But what about turning the other cheek? Confrontation isn't biblical." Isn't it? While Jesus didn't get into any fistfights, I'm sure you'll agree that He stood firm in His convictions. He verbally assaulted the religious leaders of His time, taking on a role much like that of the prophets who had warned Israel time and again to turn from its sinful ways. Jesus certainly cared enough to confront.

Sometimes changing a relationship may mean loving a person enough to say good-bye. While divorce is a very last resort, separation may be an acceptable alternative. The Bible tells us that when someone sins against us (sin being anything that is against God's will), we should:

. . . go and show him his fault, just between the two of you. If he listens to you, you have won your brother [sister, husband, wife] over. But if he will not listen, take one or two others along, so that "every matter may be established by the testimony of two or three witnesses." If he refuses to listen to them, tell it to the church; and if he refuses to listen even to the church, treat him as you would a pagan . . ." (Matthew 18:15–17 NIV).

Many of today's counselors suggest much the same method. Tell the truth in gentleness and respect. Confront when necessary. Seek counseling. Then, if no reconciliation can be made, you may need to walk away from the relationship for a time—or even forever.

Confrontation in itself has been known to work wonders. When you refuse to be a victim, when you change, often your spouse will have the impetus he or she needs to seek help.

Each individual must be willing to make the necessary changes within himself or herself in order to establish a relationship or environment that promotes love, healing, health, and respect.

Dr. James Dobson, in his book *Love Must Be Tough*, says:

Adults will occasionally challenge one another for the same reasons they challenged their parents as children. Unconsciously, perhaps, they are asking the question, "How much courage do you have, and do you love me enough to stop me from doing this foolish thing?" What they need in that moment is loving discipline that forces them to choose between good and bad alternatives. What they don't need . . . is permissiveness, understanding, excuses, removal of guilt and buckets of tender loving care. To dole out that kind of smother-love at such a time is to reinforce irresponsibility and generate disrespect. It deprives the marriage of *mutual accountability*.[1]

Dobson offers excellent advice in his book, and I'd recommend it for anyone who lacks the courage to confront in a marriage or other relationship. As we challenge a husband or wife in an effort to change damaging behavior and situations, we'll want to remain respectful and loving. Dr. Dobson goes on to give those who employ the tough-love approach some warnings:

> Remember that with God's help, you are attempting to build new bridges to this disrespectful, trapped partner. Don't burn them before they reach the other shore.

- Don't call him names, except to label his harmful behavior for what it is.
- Don't try to hurt him with gossip or even embarrassing truth.
- Don't telephone his family and try to undermine his position with them.
- Don't inflame hatred in the children of your union.
- Don't forget that your purpose is to be tough, yes, but loving as well.[2]

Recently a good Christian friend of mine, Mary, found the courage to say, "No more" to an unfaithful husband. Jeff wanted a wife, but he also wanted a mistress. After numerous broken promises and fruitless attempts at counseling, Mary filed for divorce.

"It was the hardest decision I've ever made," she told me. "The worst part was the reaction of people I thought cared about me. Although I found people who encouraged me and comforted me, it really hurt when so many 'friends' treated me like a . . . a prostitute. I've been rejected, condemned, criticized, and judged."

Mary struggled hard to find God's grace under the rubble of guilt and condemnation heaped on by her own and other people's religious ideals and false beliefs. Yet she continued to look to God as her source of strength. Since Mary's divorce, she has grown as an individual, and she has also grown spiritually. She has been able to cultivate her unique God-given talents and to turn them into a career in which she is finding fulfillment. Today she is a much stronger, more vital woman.

Did God want Mary and Jeff's marriage to end? I seriously doubt that. I think He would have preferred that her husband accept his responsibility as a man who could nurture, love, and be faithful to his wife. But that didn't happen, and the result was another shattered relationship.

Even though the results of our actions may not be what we'd like, men and women must love one another enough to say, "Wait, you're going the wrong way." And we need the courage to say, if necessary, "I love you, but unless you turn around I can't go with you."

Docking at the Temple

Without honesty to confront issues and concerns and a willingness to make changes, a relationship is likely to crumble. And it is on that note we arrive at our destination, the Temple of Doomed Relationships. Kansas ties the boat to the dock and we unload our supplies.

As we pick our way through the rubble of a once-magnificent palace where marriage was honored and cherished, we can't help but be saddened. Her laws were respected and revered as a commitment to the most high God who created her. Now they are laughed at, ignored, and broken.

In the next chapter we'll sift our way through the wreckage and see what extramarital affairs, romantic fantasies, and pornography have done to desecrate these once sacred halls.

Chapter 8
Affairs, Lust, and Other Elements of Marital Decay

"LUST," SAM MUTTERED as she threw David's clothes into his duffel bag. "Pure, unadulterated lust." That was the only explanation Sam could come up with for the failure of their marriage. They'd fallen in lust—certainly not love.

She had heard that love endured all things. If David really loved her, Sam rationalized, he'd endure staying in California.

A voice inside Sam's mind dealt a well-aimed blow to her arguments. *Love endures all things*, it said, *even Texas. You're being selfish and unfair, Samantha*. Well maybe she was, but so was he.

A knock at the door disrupted her thoughts. "Sam," David called, "are you in there?"

She hesitated, not wanting to talk with him. She had managed to avoid him all day—which isn't easy when you live on a boat!

Not hearing a response to his knock, David entered the cabin. Seeing Sam, he stopped. "I'm sorry," he said. "I didn't think you were here."

"It's okay. I . . . I was just packing your things."

"I see you're not wasting any time getting rid of me," he said gruffly.

"Well, what am I supposed to do?" she yelled. "Sit around and wait for you to change your mind?"

"Would you like me to change my mind?" his voice gentled.

Sam wanted to say yes. She wanted to tell him she had cried all night and eaten a dozen chocolate-chip cookies over him. Instead she said nothing.

"I guess I was right. You really don't love me." He took a step toward her. "But why, Sam—why did you marry me, if you didn't love me and want to spend your life with me?"

"I . . . I thought I did love you."

"And now?"

"I've decided," Sam said, "we were only physically attracted. It was nothing more than lust."

David closed the distance between them, wanting to haul Samantha into his arms and shake some sense into her. But he didn't. He held his arms stiffly at his sides. "How can you say that? What I feel for you is much more than physical. That's part of it, sure. But Sam, I love you! In fact I was even willing to give up my ranch so we could be together, but you made it pretty clear that your job came before our relationship."

"You love me?"

"Of course, I love you . . ." David growled, then stopped. The brief expression of happiness he saw in Sam's eyes restored his hope. "Sam," he said hoarsely, "you thought I didn't . . . ?"

Sam nodded her head at the man who'd become a blur. David loved her. And what was that he'd said . . . he'd give up everything for her?

David's arms went around her. Laying her head on his shoulder, she surrendered herself to him.

Hours later, Sam and David awakened in each other's arms. David's duffel bag lay in a heap on the floor as a bitter reminder of their disagreement. They would stay together. Sam felt a deep sense of joy marred only by a twinge of guilt that David had been the one to give in. Had she been selfish? Did her career and all the things it represented come first? Maybe, but now she could have both.

David held Samantha close to him. Contentment saturated him, tainted only by a tiny seed of resentment and a remnant of doubt. It still didn't seem right for him to have to give in to her. Did Sam really love him?

He scooted up in bed and gazed down at her and smiled. "Do you still think that what we have for each other is only lust?"

Sam looked into the endless blue of his eyes as if she were searching for an answer. She saw gentleness and warmth . . . and something else. Hurt? Fear? Anger? She wanted to tell him that what she felt was the kind of deep, enduring love that could sustain a marriage. But she couldn't. She wasn't even sure what that kind of love was. "I don't know," Sam said with a deep sigh. "I just don't know."

Is It Lust or Love?

Oh, dear. What's to become of our fine romance? Are David and Samantha in love or in lust? How will David respond? Will true love emerge to conquer all? I guess we'll simply have to stay tuned for the next dramatic episode to find out—or maybe we can help them work it out. To do that, let's get back to our adventure.

As you'll recall from the end of the last chapter, we have just navigated a jungle river, with Kansas as our guide, and have begun exploring the Temple of Doomed Relationships. David and Samantha didn't come along. Let's just say they were too wrapped up in each other to even notice we'd gone. But don't worry. During our temple visit we'll check in on them from time to time to see how their love story is unfolding.

Lusting After the Flesh

The jungle is hot and humid. I'm feeling an overwhelming desire for an iced tea and a cold shower. I find a shady spot in the temple ruins and lean against a fragile section of wall. I don't like this part of the expedition. All I've discovered so far are bits and pieces of pornographic literature—the ugly stuff ruined relationships are made of.

Suddenly a vulture swoops down from its perch in a nearby tree. He lands at my feet and pecks at my boot with his obscene, naked head. "Shoo!" I yell, throwing a tattered copy of an ancient *Playboy* magazine at him. "I'm not dead yet." He squawks indignantly and retreats. He sits atop one of the fragmented pillars and watches me.

Kansas walks over and hunkers down beside me. "Lustin' after the flesh, hey?"

"What?" I say, jumping to my feet. "Me? Look, Kansas, your good looks may cause women's hearts to beat a little faster, but I'm a married woman. And I am definitely not into lusting. So don't get smart with me, buster. I wrote you into this book; I can easily write you out."

"Calm down," he chuckles. "I meant the bird."

"Oh." I swallow my pride and manage a good-natured laugh at my mistake.

The analogy's a good one, though, even if it did come out of a fictional character's mouth. *Lust* is defined in *Webster's* as "1. Bodily appetite . . . excessive sexual desire . . . overmastering desire [a *lust* for power]. 2. To feel intense desire."[1] That vulture isn't interested in sex, but he sure has an appetite for the flesh!

The Demon in Sex

Many couples begin a relationship on the basis of a consuming desire for each other. If this passion is based on lust rather than love, it can work as a destructive force in a relationship. Richard Foster writes in *Money, Sex & Power*, "The demon in sex is lust. True sexuality leads to humanness, but lust leads to depersonalization. Lust captivates rather than emancipates, devours rather than nourishes."[2]

On the surface lust can look a lot like love. But lust will eventually reveal its true nature. For example, Ellen, married five years but now divorced, says, "When I met Paul I felt so loved. Here, I thought, was a man who really wanted me. I was flattered that he couldn't wait to get me into bed. He couldn't keep his hands off me. I found out later he couldn't keep his hands off a lot of other women as well. I was never a woman to him, just a sex object—a toy to play with and discard when he got bored."

We are often drawn to lust out of our basic human need for love. It is difficult to distinguish natural, God-given passion from lust.

To clarify the difference, I'd like to spend just a few minutes defining the three kinds of love that make up a marriage. Then we'll look a little more closely at how love and lust are different. As we do, consider your own relationship. Is it based more on lust or on love?

Three Loves

One of Samantha and David's problems seems to be the result of not defining their relationship more fully before they married. They certainly are not alone. A great many men and women fall in love and get married without being fully aware of their true feelings for each other.

Perhaps every premarital counseling session should include a chart on which people plot out their feelings toward each other. In fact, maybe we can do that at the end of this chapter, after we've examined the three kinds of love, which include:

• Eros . . . a romantic, sensual love, biological in nature.
• Phileo . . . a friendship love that involves sharing, communi-

cating, and working together for the good of the relationship.
• Agape . . . a spiritual or unconditional love, a consistent, commitment kind of love that endures while eros and phileo ebb
and flow.

The Fall of Eros

Many people see lust as the romantic love that brings men and
women together. But there is a difference. Romantic or erotic
love was designed by God as He created man and woman in His
image. We see evidence of it in Genesis 2:25: "And the man and
his wife were both naked and were not ashamed."

There was no need for shame because Adam and Eve shared
a mutual openness of their sexuality. They exposed themselves
physically, emotionally, and spiritually. Eros is a beautiful kind
of love that fulfills our sexual wants and desires and as such is an
exciting and pleasurable part of the marriage relationship.

Sadly, however, with the fall of Adam and Eve, eros became
contaminated. Adam and Eve felt shame and covered themselves.

Lust is the contaminant that distorts, perverts, and degrades
erotic love. Lust turns sexuality into a worship of the genitals. It
reduces intimacy to intercourse. "Lust," to borrow another
quote from Richard Foster, "produces bad sex, because it denies
relationship. Lust turns the other person into an object, a thing,
a non-person. Jesus condemned it because it cheapened sex, it
made sex less than it was created to be. For Jesus sex was too
good, too high, too holy, to be thrown away by cheap thoughts."[3]

The tragedy of lust in marriage is that we often don't recognize it until the wedding bells have rung. Then we pick up the
pieces and hope there is enough substance (enough eros, phileo,
and agape love) to glue the fragments back into a reasonable
facsimile of a marriage.

A Little Harmless Fantasy

If lust is truly a demon, we must be on guard continually lest it sink its talons deep into our souls. Its hold may begin as lightly as a feather on the shoulder, through romantic fantasies, love stories, and perhaps occasional masturbation to curb an unsatisfied sexual desire. We hardly know it's there.

Then, for some, the fantasies and stories become more intimate, more sensual, more explicit. Masturbation happens more frequently and is accompanied by lustful thoughts. The talons of lust sink deeper. These people may feel the pain and guilt of where their thoughts and readings have taken them but can't seem to—or don't want to—say no.

And then there are those for whom lust becomes a consuming passion. It creates an insatiable appetite for pornographic literature and coitus. Feeding the lust only increases the hunger. Lust can become an obsessive-compulsive drive that all too often tragically leads to sexually deviant behaviors such as rape, pedophilia, incest, adultery, masochism, and sadism.

But let's back up for a moment and take another look at those romantic fantasies and love stories. Some of you may be saying, "But I fantasize, and I sometimes read romances. Is that lust? Am I living in sin?"

Not necessarily. But if you are married and fantasizing about sex with a man other than your husband, you may want to reconsider Matthew 5:28: "Anyone who looks at a woman [man] lustfully has already committed adultery with her [him] in his [her] heart" (NIV).

That passage can be a real hindrance and guilt producer if we allow every erotic thought to saturate us with guilt. Richard Foster: "Sometimes sexual fantasies signify a longing for intimacy; at other times, they express attraction toward a beautiful and winsome person. Sexual fantasies can mean many things and we must not automatically identify them with lust."[4]

Fantasy, as I said in an earlier chapter, can be a harmless

solace and a delight—and this applies to love as well as other aspects of our lives. We can dream up romantic interludes, reminisce about that first kiss, create or enjoy romantic music and art. Foster tells us, "These are sexual events, erotic experiences, and they should not be classified as lust. . . . Perhaps one reason many couples are bored with sex is atrophy of their imagination."[5]

Still, while there may be room for romantic fantasy in our lives, we'll want to remember that the line between sexual fantasy and lust is easily crossed. In the book *Sex for Christians,* Lewis Smedes suggests a helpful way to distinguish between the two: "When a sense of excitement conceives a plan to use a person, when attraction turns into a scheme, we have crossed beyond erotic excitement into spiritual adultery."[6]

Dream Lovers: Devils in Angels' Clothing

Even when romantic fantasies aren't lustful, they can be dangerous when they create dissatisfaction with real people and real relationships. A few years ago, for instance, I went through a period in my life—I guess I'd have to call it my midlife miseries—when I became aware of an increased desire for sex. At the root of those desires was my need to be reaffirmed as an attractive and appealing woman to my husband. A couple of my writing friends were into writing romances, so I boarded the romance express and thought I'd give it a try. But to write a romance, one had to read them, so I did.

I began with a few innocent adventures from Barbara Cartland and gradually got into Harlequin® and Silhouette®. I went from one a week to one or two a day. Some were as innocent as a blush on a rose, and some even carried a message of salvation. But others were so sensual I *blushed* like a rose. I read about heroes who looked at their women as though they were the most beautiful, desirable women in the world. Women in these books burned with passion, and the all-male heroes knew just how to keep that fire alive.

Before I knew it, romantic fantasies were playing in my head. I began to wonder what it would be like to have a lover who would bring me flowers every day, always open doors for me, never complain about the moldy cheese in the refrigerator, never scold me for leaving the faucets dripping. I wondered what it would be like to have a man who would choose going to dinner with me over watching the basketball play-offs.

As I made comparisons between my husband and the domineering yet tender and gentle heroes in the books, I grew more and more aware of my husband's faults. Eventually I had to choose between Ron and the dream lovers.

I chose the real man because he has blue eyes I can see love through. He laughs and jokes with me, talks and walks with me. He touches me, hugs me, and kisses me nearly every time I need him. And he's always been faithful. (Besides, he's really a prince to love me through all my craziness, hobbies, careers, and escapades.) Real men are not perfect, and it isn't fair to a husband to be compared with a lover who doesn't exist.

Women aren't the only ones who create dream lovers, of course. Men who amuse themselves with "skin flicks" and centerfold beauties can create for themselves imaginary women with the figure and allure no real woman could match. Very few real women, especially after they've had a child or two, have flawless porcelain skin, high breasts, narrow waists—and most of us would look ridiculous in bunny tails. (Even models themselves don't look that good in real life!) Real women sometimes act frazzled, break out in zits, gain weight, sink into moods, wrinkle, and develop gray hair just as men do.

Dream lovers, I have decided, are devils in angels' clothing. They appeal to our senses, titillate and tease us, but when we reach out to hold them they disappear. They offer us fulfillment beyond our wildest fantasies, but once we believe in them, dream lovers taunt us and fill us with discontentment and regret.

Dream lovers claim they can fill the empty places in our hearts where no human man or woman can reach. They claim to feed our soul hunger. But I have found that dream lovers offer only a momentary illusion of fullness. When the moment passes, the emptiness and soul hunger are greater than ever before.

Romantic fantasies may be harmless in small and occasional doses. But they, like drugs and alcohol, can become an addiction that eventually leads to a full-blown, sin-ridden life of dissatisfaction, lust, affairs, and crumbled relationships.

No One Is Immune

How is your love life? We all have vulnerable times when we can easily slip over the brink into the abyss called lust. The sad part is that none of us, no matter how strong or spiritual we think we are, is immune to temptations of sexual immorality.

"Me?" you may be saying, "Never!"

I've heard it said that today's men and women are too sophisticated and street smart to get caught in the web of fantasy, mystery, romance, and dead-end relationships. I've also heard Christians claim they are above sexual temptation and would never have an affair.

Randy Alcorn, in his book *Christians in the Wake of the Sexual Revolution*, clearly disputes that claim:

Make no mistake about it—the Christian church is riddled with immorality, among the young and older, the single and the married, the laity and the leadership. No Christian is immune to sexual temptation. We do ourselves no favor to pretend that the same hormones and human weaknesses common to all people are somehow eradicated when we come to Christ.[7]

I've never had an affair, and I'm firmly committed to my husband, but that doesn't mean it could never happen. During my midlife struggle, when I began reading romances, I also realized I was in an extremely vulnerable position. There were times I felt isolated, lonely, and in desperate need of reassurance. Given the right circumstances and a slightly different set of values, I could easily have become involved with someone else.

Being aware of the possibility and understanding the ramifications of an affair, I was always careful to keep my friendships with men on a purely platonic level. I consider myself fortunate, however, and when I hear of others falling into the snare of affairs and adultery, I don't feel I can point an accusing finger. I simply have to say to myself, "There but for God's grace go I."

Why Do Affairs Happen?

Most people who have affairs don't intentionally go out looking for them. An affair may begin as an innocent friendship or work relationship.

Marie, for example, met Larry at a church retreat. "I didn't intend to become involved with Larry," she says. "It just happened. We were paired up to work on a fund-raiser, and . . . we became close friends. We could talk about everything. My husband wasn't a Christian, and I loved the way Larry and I could spend hours discussing spiritual issues. . . . He made me feel important, intelligent. We were so emotionally and spiritually attuned. It just seemed natural to move into the physical realm, too. Larry understood me—loved me—something my husband stopped doing years ago."

Marie wasn't looking for a clandestine affair, but her emotional, spiritual, and physical needs were going unmet. She became involved with her lover because he was able—if only temporarily—to fill those empty places inside.

Then again, some affairs are more deliberately planned by men and women who rationalize that if needs, particularly in the sexual area, aren't met at home, they must be met elsewhere. Some claim that affairs keep their marriages exciting. There are even cases in which psychologists have advocated extramarital affairs in lieu of divorce.

Some of the rationalizations are based on the assumption that we *need* sex. But the apostle Paul soundly refutes that claim: "You cannot say that our physical body was made for sexual promiscuity; it was made for the Lord, and in the Lord is the answer to its needs" (1 Corinthians 6:13 PHILLIPS).

Randy Alcorn concurs: "While other urges exist for our physical maintenance," he points out, "sex does not. We will die without food and water. We will not die without sex. Sex is never an emergency, immorality never a necessity. Lust, however, tells us otherwise."[8]

An affair, no matter how appealing it may be or how innocently it starts, is a sin, and as such it comes with an often high and painful price. Unfortunately, the price is paid not only by those who engage in the affair but also by the victims—the innocent husbands or wives who have been wronged. I don't have to tell you about the cover-ups, the lies, the deceit, the lost trust, the guilt, and the broken hearts that affairs bring; it is clearly written on divorce decrees all over the country. Like drugs, affairs may bring a temporary high, but eventually the users drop to earth and find their lives in shambles.

How do we safeguard our relationships from attacks of lust and the damage of affairs? You can prevent your romance from becoming another artifact in the Temple of Doomed Relationships. Here are some ideas:

- Be aware of the pitfalls. Know the temptations are there for wives as well as husbands, and no one is exempt.
- Examine your marriage fortress for possible broken or cracked sections. Are there vulnerable areas that Satan with his partner, lust, can break through?
- Communicate with one another about concerns in this area. Stabilize your marriage by verbalizing your needs, then work toward meeting those needs as much as possible.

- Pray for one another (or pray with a friend) for protection against those temptations and for the strength to walk away.
- Confess your sexually immoral thoughts and actions to someone (perhaps a pastor) whom you can trust not to break confidentiality.
- Say no. Walk away from and deal honestly with sexual temptations. Author Lois Mowday tells us, "For the person in an affair to continue having contact with the adulterous partner is like the alcoholic's 'one more drink.' I counsel going cold turkey, and I think that's the only way it works."[9]

Relationships built on erotic love alone are more likely to crumble under the influence of lust. In order to survive sexual temptation, marriages need strong levels of all three kinds of love.

Physical attraction is wonderful, but it becomes empty without the sustaining power of friendship (phileo love). Friendship—the ability to laugh and cry together—gives a relationship stability and warmth. Phileo love is deep and bonding—essential to a marriage.

Especially important is agape, which is an unconditional love that transcends all the problems, temptations, disillusionments, and misunderstandings of a marriage.

Author Judith Viorst touches on the meaning of agape love as she describes the difference between real love and infatuation:

Infatuation is when you think that he's as gorgeous as Robert Redford, as pure as Solzhenitsyn, as funny as Woody Allen, as athletic as Jimmy Connors, and as smart as Albert Einstein. Love is when you realize that he's as gorgeous as Woody Allen, as smart as Jimmy Connors, as funny as Solzhenitsyn, as athletic as Albert Einstein, and nothing like Robert Redford in any category—but you'll take him anyway.[10]

Agape love is permanent, intense, respectful, and it is not altered by the on-and-off emotions of romance.

Charting Your Love Life

Earlier I suggested we'd have a chance to plot the levels of love in our own relationships. Personal Inventory 5 consists of two identical graphs for you to use in any way you choose. You may want to fill out one for how your relationship was in the beginning and do a comparison with the current love levels. You may want to do the first, then ask your partner to fill in the second, and compare notes. If you're single and not involved in a relationship, you may want to either skip this or measure the love components of your last relationship.

Personal Inventory 5
Love Levels Chart

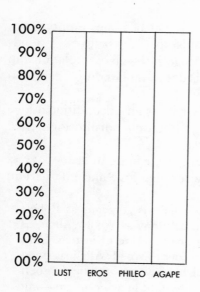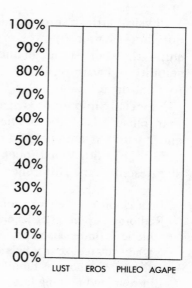

To complete the graphs, simply draw a horizontal line in each section indicating what percent of your relationship you think is based on lust, erotic or romantic love, phileo or friendship love, and unconditional agape love. (Be sure your totals come to 100 percent!)

As an example, let's look at the love levels of our storybook couple, David and Samantha. First, agape love. Both David and Sam have a sense of commitment to the marriage, but each is insecure. Before their difficulty, they intended that their love last forever. David perhaps can claim a higher level of agape because, even though he doesn't like it, he's willing to give up part of himself for Sam. Also, remember that he didn't press for sexual involvement before marriage. Agape love involves respect and restraint regardless of sexual attraction. I'd give David a 15 percent level of agape and Sam 10 percent. It's not a lot; but this kind of love takes time to grow and mature.

Phileo love comes next. Although Sam and David have some things in common, they have not as yet been together long enough to develop a deep friendship. I'd have to give both 5 percent in phileo love.

Eros? I'd give Sam 65 percent and David 75 percent in that area. Until recently, their heads were in the stars, and most of their relationship at this time is based on physical attraction.

As for lust, I'd say because of Sam's determination to find the perfect mate by depersonalizing humans to computer specifications and basing David's sexual performance on novels she's read, she's up to 20 percent in lust. David, we must admit, did lust after Samantha's body and was rather obsessive about rushing her into marriage, but he always treated her with respect. I'd rate his lust level at 5 percent.

How did you do? I have to admit that when Ron and I first got married, our eros level was right up there with Sam and David's. Now however, phileo, agape, and eros have pretty much equal billing. Lust weighs in at only about 3 percent. While this isn't a scientific study, it can help us see where we stand and pinpoint areas of our love life that need work.

And it does take work. For Ron and me, the road has been a

difficult one. Commitment isn't cheap. The walls around our marriage have been broken and patched up more times than I'd care to remember.

Here at the Temple of Doomed Relationships, I pick my way through the rubble and struggle to make sense of how sexual temptations and immorality can do so much damage to relationships. I'm saddened that something so beautiful, so fulfilling, pleasant, fun, and exciting as sex can be turned into a devouring monster called lust.

It appears that what men and women need in one another is a balance of eros, phileo, and agape love, along with an awareness of the dangers of lust and a willingness to say no. The last things any of us need are lust, dream lovers, and affairs.

I know you're as anxious as I am to find out about David and Samantha, so we're going to move into the next chapter now, where we'll see whether or not our couple can patch up their crumbling marriage. We'll also be resuming our exploration of the temple to locate artifacts of the greatest marriage killer of them all—divorce.

Chapter 9
The Trouble With Divorce

IN THE LAST CHAPTER, David and Samantha had partially resolved one argument and were heading for another. As you'll recall, Samantha wasn't sure whether she was really in love with David.

David was stunned at Samantha's response. So stunned, in fact, that after ten minutes we still find him staring at the ceiling as if he expects to read his answers there. The only thing he knows for certain is that their relationship is in deep trouble.

"Sam." David turned to his side and stroked her cheek.

"Hmmm?"

"I'm trying hard to understand where you're coming from. But how can you relegate all those beautiful moments we've shared to the degrading status of lust? I *know* I love you. I want you with me forever."

Samantha wanted David forever, too. And who was she to decide what love was, anyway? All the books she had read surely didn't help. And her parents . . . that couldn't have been love. "David," she asked, "how can you be so sure that what we have is love?"

David shrugged. "I don't know. I just know how I feel. Love

isn't happy all the time, you know. I mean, there's bound to be fights and times when you wonder if you did the right thing by getting married. When I met you, I felt as if my world had turned upside down. It didn't take a computer to show me you were the girl I wanted to marry."

"It didn't?"

"No." David turned her around to face him. "From the minute I saw you, I wanted to run my fingers through that long, thick hair of yours and kiss those adorable lips. And when I looked into your eyes, I knew I was gone. What I felt then was purely physical attraction, I know, but the more we talked and did things together, the more I was convinced you were the woman I wanted to spend the rest of my life with."

"But you didn't tell me you loved me until after I ran our names through the computer."

"You'd never have believed me. I figured I'd just have to . . . ah . . . wait . . . for the computer to put us together."

"But the computer *did* put—unless . . ." Sam pushed David back onto the bed and sat up. "Oh, David, you didn't . . . you didn't."

"What?" David asked.

"You tampered with the computer . . . you—you sabotaged it . . ."

"Sam." He reached out to grasp her arms. She pushed him away. "Okay, but it's no big deal. All I did was look at your data base and write some things on mine that would jibe. Is that a crime?"

"Yes!" she yelled. "It is. How could you do this to me? I had it all figured out. My computer would select a man who would be ideally suited to me. Then you came along and . . . oh, just go away. I never want to see you again."

"You don't mean that. We're married, for Pete's sake. We love each other. That computer business is a bunch of hogwash, anyway. People shouldn't be reduced to a bunch of facts and figures."

"Hogwash?" Sam shrilled. She had devised a way for people to skip all the dating and searching, fighting and divorcing, and find the right person, and David was dismissing it as nothing more than a silly game.

"It's cold and calculating, that's what it is! And I was not about to trust a computer with the rest of my life. I admit, I signed on with the ship and agreed to be analyzed, but I was getting frustrated. Then, when we met, I didn't need a machine to help me find a woman to love. It isn't natural, Sam. We didn't need it."

"*I* needed it. It was the only way for me, David. Don't you see that? I had to have some way to be sure I wasn't making a mistake . . ."

"Couldn't you have trusted your heart, Sam? Everybody knows when they fall in love."

"No! I don't. I trusted my heart to my father and mother. Daddy would say he loved me and tell me I was his precious little girl, then the next thing I knew he'd rip up the house and hit Mom and me. She would try to protect me. And sometimes I thought she loved me. But she stayed—she stayed with him . . ." Tears flowed freely down Sam's cheeks and she didn't bother to wipe them away. "Don't you see? If she had really loved me, she would have left him. So you tell me, how am I supposed to know what love really is when nobody ever loved me?"

"Sam . . ." David reached for her, wanting to comfort her and protect her from the hurts of her past, but she backed away. He could almost see the wall go up around her as she straightened. They were in real trouble here, and he didn't know how to deal with it.

"No, David, just leave it alone. Computers don't lie—only people do."

"So you put your trust in a piece of machinery? Look, maybe I shouldn't have manipulated the data from your questionnaire. But I thought if we could just have some time together, you'd see that, computer or no, we were meant to be together. I'm not a perfect man; you'll never find that, Sam. But I love you and I'll do whatever it takes to prove it to you. I'd never treat you like your father did. We could have a terrific marriage if we just work on it."

She wasn't listening. Frustrated, David ran his fingers through his hair and took a step toward her. "Don't throw it away," he pleaded.

"There's nothing left to throw away!"

The stubborn set to Samantha's jaw told him that further argument would be useless. "I never would have believed anybody could be so cold." Quiet fury exploded within him. He retrieved his clothes and stuffed them in the bag. "Don't worry, Sam, I won't bother you again." He tossed the words over his shoulder as he walked out.

"Fine," she heard herself shouting at David's retreating figure. "Just leave. I'll call my lawyer and ask him to draw up the divorce papers in the morning and mail them to you."

The door slammed. He was gone. Sam ran to the door, fully intending to yank it open and call him back, but she didn't. He had mocked her software program—her whole life's work. Worse, he had lied to her. She was lucky to be rid of him. If she was so lucky, why did the thought of his leaving bring so much pain? Sam shuffled to the bed and curled up under the covers. She rocked, willing the hurt to go away. A memory pushed its way to the surface of her mind. She was twelve years old. Her father had walked out, and Mom had gone after him. In her mind she heard their hollow steps on the old wooden porch. She was alone—would always be alone.

Is This the End?

I sure hope David and Samantha don't end up in divorce court. But I guess we'll have to wait until the next episode to find out. Oh, my. You'll have to excuse me a minute while I blow my nose. I always cry at stories with unhappy endings. And nothing creates a more unhappy ending for a marriage than divorce. I agree with Chuck Swindoll, who wrote that "two processes ought never be entered into prematurely: embalming and divorce."[1] Now with those words in mind, it's time to return to our jungle outing.

Haunting Memories

Midnight haunts the Temple of Doomed Relationships. Kansas has doused the campfire and everyone has bedded down in their hammocks for the night. "Get some rest," he says. "We've got a full day tomorrow. And," Kansas flashes us a wicked grin, "you might hear moaning and crying during the night. Nothing to worry about. It'll just be the ghosts of dead relationships." He chuckles as he blows out the last lantern. "Sleep tight."

I shiver, doubting I'll be able to sleep at all. Ghosts, indeed! A full, pale blue moon illuminates the temple ruins and casts eerie black shadows over the landscape. I feel cold inside, empty, haunted by memories of marriages gone bad.

My mind conjures up a vision of a couple slipping into quicksand, eyes filled with bitterness and hate. I call to them but they don't answer. "Be careful," I warn them as they sink deeper and deeper into the bottomless pit. "Reach out for help!" I yell. "You don't have to let it end this way . . ." Still they won't listen. I stretch out my hand to them. They ignore it. I stand there helpless, aching to bring them back. They disappear under the surface . . .

"No, no," I hear myself cry. "Not another one."

"Hey," a voice calls from far away. "You all right?"

I wake up in a cold sweat. "What?"

"You were crying out in your sleep," Kansas says. "Must have been having a nightmare. Want to tell me about it?"

"Yes." I tell him about the couple sinking in quicksand and my feelings of helplessness. "Such a strange dream," I muse. "People don't die in divorce."

"No," he murmurs thoughtfully. "But a part of them does." He stares absently into the night and walks away. And I realize my vision has shown me the harsh and painful truth. I close my eyes and think of all the people I know whose relationships have died. One memory comes through especially clear . . . perhaps because I feel it never should have happened.

"I'm Leaving . . ."

At thirty-six, my friend Sharie left the man she had been married to for fifteen years.

"It's over. I'm leaving John—for good," she told me over the phone.

"Oh, Sharie," I stammered, hoping the finality in her voice didn't really signify the end of their relationship. I didn't want to hear this. "Are you sure? I mean, divorce is such a big step. Maybe you could try going to a counselor first."

"No. My mind is made up. I've been thinking about it for a long time, so don't try to talk me out of it. I'm going to see the lawyer this afternoon."

"What happened?" I asked, thinking that perhaps if she calmed down she might rethink her decision.

"Nothing specific. He came home from work and plopped himself in front of the television set. I wanted to talk to him. I just *needed* him to hold me, to reassure me. 'Not now, honey,' he says, 'can't you see the news is on?' If it's not the news it's some cop show or sports thing. He never wants to talk. And when His Royal Highness finally acquiesces to allow me an audience, he still doesn't really listen. I swear he loves that television set more than he ever loved me. Sometimes I wish he were having an affair with another woman—at least with her I could offer some competition."

She hesitated. I didn't know what to say. I could understand only too well her need to be listened to—to be appreciated, loved; to have a companion instead of a couch potato. I also understood his need for a quiet time—a time to unwind, to catch up on world events, to lose himself in a place free of pressures and responsibilities. I thought of telling her to put herself in his place, but I didn't. I wanted to talk her out of her decision, but I didn't. As a counselor I knew that about the only option I had at that moment, if I really wanted to be her friend, was to meet at least one of her needs—to listen to her.

Sharie sighed. "Look, I'm sorry for venting on you. It's just . . . I have been waiting for years for that man to change. I've tried being warm and cuddly; I've tried assertiveness and fighting fair—nothing works. I've read my last marriage book. I'm sick and tired of treading softly and constantly having to be on guard so I don't upset him. He can be as cranky as a wounded rhinoceros."

"Where will you go?" I asked. "What about the children?" Her daughters were in their teens and I knew how devastated they'd be.

"I don't know . . . we'll probably move out to Mother's for a few days until I can find an apartment. We'll manage. Anything will be better than living one more day with that—that bum."

"Are you sure this is what you want?"

"No . . . it's not what I want. What I want is to be happy—with John. Just once, I'd like to feel as if I mean something more to him than a person who does his laundry, feeds him, and gives him sex on demand. I want to feel loved and cherished and . . . but it's not going to happen, and I've decided to stop kidding myself."

"It isn't going to be easy," I said. I wanted to fix it for her, wished there was something I could do—some witty and wise statement I could make to change her mind and to make both of them more alert to each other's needs.

"I know, but what else can I do? He obviously doesn't love

151

me and I . . . I don't feel *anything* right now. He probably won't even notice I'm gone until he's hungry."

"Sharie, before you take the final steps, please see a counselor. Your problems aren't hopeless. Maybe you can work things out."

"Well, maybe, but I doubt it will change anything."

And it didn't.

There's No Such Thing as a Painless Divorce

I should take a moment to tell you that I am in no way condemning or judging men and women who have opted for divorce. As I've mentioned before, I do believe there are times when divorce may be the only alternative. I have a number of friends who divorced to escape abuse, an addictive spouse, severe emotional battering, abandonment, or adultery. But no matter what the circumstances, divorce brings with it the pain and grief of a significant loss.

More and more people are recognizing that the common wisdom of the past several decades—divorce is a relatively painless cure for incompatibility and problems in living together—*is simply not true.* Yet each year large numbers of men and women still choose to go their separate ways without being fully aware of the serious consequences of their decision. Oh, we know that divorce is unpleasant, but we talk ourselves into believing we'd be better off divorced than to continue living in what we see as a dead marriage. "When a marriage is dead, bury it" seems the logical thing to do. But as writer David Neff points out, ". . . The longer we live with the aftermath of divorce, the more we come to realize that no relationship ever fully dies, and that for family members—children in particular—divorce can feel like burying not the dead, but the terminally ill."[2]

I'd be lying if I told you I've never considered divorce. In an earlier chapter I shared how at one point in my marriage I'd become terribly disillusioned and depressed. For a time, running away from home sounded like a good idea. Like most people, I considered the benefits. My fantasy of life alone included having less laundry to do, being responsible for and to no one but myself, living a life without television, and just being alone sometimes. Being a writer, I desperately need private space, and with a husband and children around I never seemed to be able to get enough of it.

It was only when I forced myself to look at the pain, the loneliness, and to weigh what I might gain against what I would lose, that I opted to stay in my marriage and work it out.

Many of us imagine that we'll be able to overcome the difficulties and tend to picture ourselves enjoying the good times. Novels and television shows paint an appealing picture of people (including children) who not only survive divorce but also go on to live happier, more well-adjusted lives. We think that, like them, we will just shed a few tears, straighten our shoulders, walk tall, and walk out. Lawyers offer quick, easy, and cheap divorces on their television ads, reducing divorce to the magnitude of trading in a used car. The truth is, divorce hurts a lot more than we'd like to believe.

How much? I have never been divorced, so I cannot speak firsthand about what it is like. Yet that doesn't mean I don't have some understanding of the pain it brings. Just as we can comprehend the idea that a hot stove burns without actually touching it, we can gain some insight as to the dangers of divorce without going through one.

"Divorce Is a Taste of Hell"

In the Bible, God expresses His feelings about divorce in unequivocal terms: " 'For I hate divorce,' says the Lord God of Israel" (Malachi 2:16). I believe that God makes this statement not to lay down an immutable law but to protect us—because, as many are discovering, divorce is not liberating but hurtful to us. In a sense, God is saying, "Don't touch that fire. I love you too much to see you get burned."

Dale Evans Rogers, who experienced divorce early in her life, vividly describes the experience as "a taste of hell. No matter how you slice it, no matter who is to blame, it can only be defined as failure to fulfill a contract between two people. In a sense, it is almost like the feeling of losing a part of yourself in death."[3]

Many people have told me that divorce can be likened to losing a spouse or a child to death. But perhaps even more basic is the analogy of losing an arm or a leg. In marriage a bonding takes place that physically, spiritually, and emotionally makes two people one. This is one of the mysteries of our human sexuality. In Genesis we see part of the mystery revealed as Adam claims his wife, saying, "This is now bone of my bones, And flesh of my flesh . . ." (2:23). In marriage, ". . . A man will leave his father and mother and be united to his wife, and they will become one flesh" (v. 24 NIV).

Consider the Children

Divorce has no respect for age. In fact, the most seriously injured victims of divorce are the most vulnerable—the children.

Recent studies have shown that even after ten years, many children of divorce still suffer from depression, poor relationship with one or both parents, feelings of rejection, and inability to trust. Many of these children go into adulthood unable to form lasting bonds, still dragging along emotional baggage such as fear, sadness, anger, guilt, and grief.[4]

"Even when children experience an immediate sense of relief because parental squabbles have been cut off," says writer David Neff, "the sense of abandonment can be crippling."[5]

A Case for Working Things Out

In recent years there has been a change in attitude among psychologists, psychiatrists, counselors, and other helping professionals regarding divorce. Today, many counselors who once would have suggested divorce as the best option are promoting marital and family therapy in an effort to keep families together. In cases where divorce does happen, they are putting much greater effort into seeing that the children's emotional needs are met.

One such counselor is Diane Medved, author of *A Case Against Divorce,* who admits, "I've helped plenty of struggling couples through separation and 'liberation.' I originally thought that staying together in turmoil was more traumatic than making the break, that striking down taboos about divorce was part of modern enlightenment. I was wrong."

Medved goes on to say, "Treating divorce as 'morally neutral'—an option no better or worse than staying married—was irreparably damaging to the very people I wanted to help."[6]

Unfortunately, even with the changing trends, it is estimated that one million couples a year head for the divorce courts. And even with all the self-help books on choosing the right mate, communicating, and loving oneself and others, therapists who counsel married couples still hear the same old stories. Most marriages end as a result of:

- ineffective methods of communication.
- inability to resolve conflict.
- sexual dissatisfaction.
- unrealistic goals and expectations.
- unresolved conflicts of the past.
- financial problems.
- differing ideas on child rearing.

Sadly, nearly all these reasons people give for divorcing a mate can, if the couple is willing, be worked out.

Some of you may be saying, "I don't want a reconciliation. I'd never go back into that situation." And you may be right. As I've said before, there are circumstances where divorce may be a viable alternative. But even then, it is important to work through the problems that led to the split.

Working through problems and being reconciled doesn't necessarily mean remarrying or even staying with the person you're in a relationship with. Rather, as you'll see in Part 3 of this book, it means learning to live in harmony with God, with yourself, and with others. And that is something all men and women—married or single—need to learn.

But for now we must leave the ghosts of dead relationships behind, as dawn spreads a golden canopy across the jungle. We awaken to the scent of fresh coffee and bacon. "What's on the agenda today?" I ask our guide.

Kansas smiles. "Last night, just before dusk, I stumbled upon an underground chamber. I suspect it will hold important evidence as to why so many marriages end up here in the Temple of Doomed Relationships."

"That's wonderful," I say. "I can hardly wait to get into the next chapter to discover the inside story."

Oh, but before we climb into the temple's depths, let's check on David and Samantha. After their argument, David had radioed for a helicopter to pick him up. He didn't talk to Sam—didn't see any point. But he did leave her this note:

My Dearest Samantha,

I'm sorry about the computer. My only excuse is that I wanted you. Perhaps it's best if we separate for a few days to think about what each of us wants to do with our lives. I'm certain we can work things out. You may find it hard to trust me after what happened, but I hope you will try.

I'll be back by the time you dock in Reconciliation Bay. Count on it.

All my love, David

Chapter 10
Secrets of the Past

Dawn greeted Samantha with glowing colors, but she acknowledged it with a scowl. She had awakened with a terrible headache, her eyes red and puffy as a result of a fitful night of tears. "I should be happy he's gone," Sam told herself. "He's a rat, a jerk, and I never want to see him again."

Even as the brave words escaped her lips, she knew deep inside they weren't true. An aching loneliness grew within her, and instead of feeling relief at David's absence, she felt only pain. A part of her was missing. He had deserted her.

But Sam, a gentle voice inside reminded her, *you sent him away.*

"He would have left anyway," she argued firmly. "I'm not the kind of person people stay with." She knew now that she cared deeply for David, even if he had interfered with her computer program. Now that she thought about it, David's schemes—his deception to win her over, the helicopter he had ordered to bring roses and a ring—testified that he cared for her. And Samantha could never remember being wanted before.

"Give us a chance," David had said. Maybe she should give

him another chance to prove his love. "I'll be back," his note had said. But would he? Maybe all these moves to win her were for show—a way to get what he wanted. . . . *No,* she decided, *not David.*

Determined to believe him, Samantha forced the hurtful memories back into the far corners of her mind. As she showered, dressed, and straightened the suite, she let her mind linger on the sweetness of David's kisses, the gentle warmth of his caress, the love she had seen reflected in his eyes. David *would* come back. And this time she would be whatever he wanted her to be, do whatever he wanted to do. She would try to make it work!

Morning found David Hartley in his home in the Texas Panhandle—and in an excessively foul mood. He hadn't slept all night, and the tangled and twisted sheets on his bed attested to his restlessness. The questions he had tried to put out of his mind assaulted him again. Could their marriage really be over? How could he bring Sam to her senses? What did he have to do to prove he loved her?

He'd been convinced a separation was what they both needed; now he wasn't so sure. He'd played his cards as best he could. But this was no race, no piece of property on which he could negotiate. Sam was a woman over whose actions and thoughts he had no control. Sam turned him inside out. She had him feeling things he'd never felt before. And David didn't like it one bit. Neither did he take kindly to the idea of explaining to his mother why he'd come back from a honeymoon without a wife!

He dressed quickly in his jeans and a western-cut shirt, then pulled on his boots. Not wanting to face the questions in his mother's eyes, he slipped quietly down an outdoor stairway and headed for the barn. Maybe a ride on Jennie would ease his mind or at least help him sort things out—at least she was a female he could depend on.

As David raced his horse across a field of wildflowers, he

gained a sense of peace and power he hadn't felt since meeting Samantha. It felt good to be home again. David gave his aching heart up to the wind, which gently caressed and comforted him as he and his chestnut mare thundered over the Texas plains.

When he neared the steep cliff walls of Pale Horse Canyon, he pulled up the reins and Jennie danced, tossing her head as if to protest the end of an exhilarating run. David eased his horse along a narrow ridge that led down into the gorge. As the horse and rider inched along, hugging the wall, David heard a familiar sound and froze. Slowly, quietly, he eased his rifle from its saddle holster. But before he could take aim and fire, the rattler struck at Jennie's leg. The mare bolted and lost her footing. Both horse and rider plunged down the canyon onto the rocks below.

It's Always Darkest Before the Dawn

Will dawn ever come again for David? He had promised to return to Samantha in two days. Now even if we do find the source of David and Samantha's inner problems, it may be too late. But for their sake, and for the sake of brokenhearted lovers everywhere, we have to try.

It may be obvious to you that much of Samantha's trouble relating to her spouse comes as a result of a childhood in which she was abused and abandoned. At times her emotional needs exceed her ability to reason. Within her is a wounded child who resists love for fear of abandonment. Yet her need to be loved and wanted duels with that fear, leaving her confused and vulnerable.

David, were we to psychoanalyze him, would present a slightly different picture. His problems run as deep and he isn't even aware of their presence. He was raised to be a man's man— tough, unemotional, in control. He's not a quitter. But he is very uncomfortable with the feelings of tenderness Sam has awakened in him.

David has spent his whole life trying to be the kind of man he thought his father (who died when David was ten) would have wanted him to be, but David feels he has never quite succeeded. Now, once again—this time in his relationship with Sam—he hasn't measured up. A real man would never let a woman dictate where they would settle down!

David is trapped in a false illusion that he must somehow follow in the footsteps of the invincible, in-control hero a ten-year-old imagined his father to be. A part of David was lost or stifled when his father died and he took on the role of "man of the house." Through no fault of his parents, David was an abandoned child. He never grieved the death of his father; he simply stepped in to take his place.

David and Samantha are like millions of couples today. They are incomplete, fragmented people searching for something—someone—to make them whole. They each carry around within them a hurting child who has never been allowed to heal. The most serious problems they face are unresolved conflicts of the past involving such matters as 1) family patterns, roles, and rules; 2) a struggle for wholeness; 3) the loss of self; and 4) the inner wounded child.

Journey to the Dark Places of the Mind

To examine more closely the problems of the past and the internal confusion that can seriously affect our relationships, let's turn our imaginations back to the Temple of Doomed Relationships. We're about to step into the dark, damp basement of our existence, wherein lie the unseen, often unnoticed causes of failed marriages. With flashlights in hand, we follow Kansas through the black opening in the temple's floor. Darkness swallows us as we descend a long, winding, narrow flight of stairs.

"Here we are," Kansas says through gritted teeth as he pushes a heavy door aside. The air is stifling and musty. We enter a large square room. Giant cobwebs sway like hammocks from the water-stained, brown granite walls. Around us are piled boxes stuffed with toys. I see teddy bears, dolls, wagons, bikes—the stuff childhood memories are made of.

"What does all this mean?" I ask.

"This is the past." Kansas sweeps the beam of his light around the room. "These are the things that make us what we are."

Put the Past Behind You

Why does the past affect us so much? We are adults. We should be able to put past hurts behind us and live in the here and now. Even the Bible says we should "forget the former things" and "not dwell on the past" (Isaiah 43:18 NIV). But while the concept of leaving the past behind sounds reasonable and may be desirable, it is not easy.

When we are young and in love, few of us stop to analyze what each individual brings into the relationship. We grow up and marry, seldom stopping to consider the impact the memories, learned behavior patterns, attitudes, family and cultural rules, and past injuries can have on our present relationships. But then, in a flash of recognition, we see ourselves responding to a memory instead of a mate, or acting just as our parents might have in an argument, or living according to rules we're not even conscious of.

For some of us, thinking about the past brings brutal reminders of times we'd just as soon forget; we don't want to dredge up those old hurts. But even when we feel we've managed to put those painful yesterdays behind us, certain feelings and memories escape from their hiding places deep within our souls, bitterly reminding us that the past won't be dismissed quite so readily.

So how do we put the past behind us? It may seem crazy, but in many instances we cannot forget the past and go on with our lives until we *remember* the past, deal with it, and learn from it.

Sometimes we must remember wrong things we have done

and bring them into the present so they can be confessed and forgiven. At other times we may need to remember events so we can forgive others. Then, too, we may want to look at the past to help us live more fully in the present and avoid making mistakes in the future.

"For everything that was written in the past was written to teach us, so that through endurance and encouragement of the Scriptures we might have hope" (Romans 15:4 NIV). The past can provide a key as to why we act the way we do. In that knowledge we can allow our memories, however painful, to teach us better and more effective ways of relating to people.

All in the Family

Deep in the musty temple bowels, I shine my spotlight on an old, wooden trunk. The lid is secured by rusty hinges that creak as I lift it. The trunk is full of pictures—hundreds of photographs of relatives, reunions, children, families. Rolled up in one corner is a piece of parchment—a genealogical record.

I can guess why the family tree is here. Our family systems play a major role in who we are and what we bring into a marriage partnership. Yet how often do we hear the line:

"I'm not marrying your family, I'm marrying you. The way our parents live has nothing to do with us."

Wrong. We are each born into a family system that becomes part of us. When we marry, no matter how separated we think we are, we bring that system with us. During the romantic phase of our relationship we are often too much in love to recognize the family differences because we are too intent on pleasing each other. After marriage, however, the scene usually changes dramatically. It is estimated that a couple spends the first ten years of married life adjusting to each other's differences—and many of those differences are rooted in family systems.

For example, the other day my pastor said, "In my family, my mother always used to take out the garbage. In my wife's family, her father had the job. When we first got married, we argued about whose job it should be. The garbage sat there for four days. I finally gave in and did it, because I couldn't stand the smell anymore. In *our* family, it became my job."

You can probably think of many examples like that one. I can. Ron's family celebrates Christmas on Christmas Day—mine, on Christmas Eve. In *our* family, we celebrate both days.

His mother made spaghetti sauce that simmered all day. I made mine in twenty minutes, and after a few years Ron stopped complaining and decided mine was just as good.

He ruined my perfectly seasoned scrambled eggs by dousing them with catsup. He still does, and I still wince!

My mother never worked outside the home. His mother did. So did I.

My parents never got a divorce. His parents did . . . and the differences go on and on.

A family tree is much more than faded photographs, and we can significantly reduce marital conflict if we remember to sort through our family history before we marry—or at least before we ask for a divorce.

I had reminisced about the family heritage long enough, so I closed the lid of the musty old chest and moved on.

In Search of Wholeness

The next item to catch my flashlight beam is a portrait on the wall. A woman. "But this is crazy," I mutter to myself. "She's only half there, and I can't tell who she is." I cock my head and wonder what significance this half person has in our search for elements that undermine and destroy relationships.

"Puzzled?" Kansas asks, coming to stand behind me.

"Yes, it seems that some very essential parts of this lady are missing."

"Ah," Kansas nods, "but I suspect she's like so many people who wander through life expecting they'll someday meet their other half. She needs a man to complete the picture."

"That's silly," I say. "If you were to put half a man next to her, you wouldn't have a whole picture; you'd just have a more ridiculous-looking portrait of two half people."

"Hmmm." Kansas smiles knowingly. "So what you're saying is that two halves don't necessarily make a whole."

Exactly. Have you ever said or heard someone make the philosophical comment that goes like this: "We were like two half souls searching the universe for our other part, and now we'll be united as one."

Could it be that relationships fail partly because what we want in a mate is often based on what we wish we could find within ourselves? To compensate for our weakness, we choose a person we feel is strong. We look for someone to fill our empty places—to heal our childhood wounds of abandonment, mistrust, inadequacy.

We marry for completeness. Unfortunately, instead of finding our missing part and being healed, we usually find that our wounds grow wider and deeper because we both need what the other can't give—what perhaps no human being can give.

Author, lecturer, and theologian John Bradshaw, who has written and spoken extensively on what he calls the "dysfunctional family system," writes:

When people marry out of deficiency and incompleteness . . . the relationship is headed for trouble. Each needs the other for completion. In courtship each is willing to *give* because of the long range fantasy that by *giving* each will ultimately *get* the other to complete them. This giving to get is one of the most troublesome and deceptive dynamics in relationships. Giving to get is a counterfeit form of love . . . each *needy* partner is conned by the illusion that the other is actually going to fulfill their incomplete self.[1]

I well understand what Bradshaw is talking about. Ron and I, like so many couples, first came together feeling we'd found our other half. The physical and emotional "oneness" of love and marriage made us feel as though we had also become whole in our identities. That sense of unity is very real, but it is only a diversion. The temporary joy and insanity of romance exceeds the pain and emptiness of the missing self, but only for a time.

For us, two half identities did not merge into one whole. Rather, we were like two separate parts who crashed into each other and splintered. All too soon, we had become thorns in each other's flesh. Fortunately, we've stayed together and continued to work out our differences in our move toward wholeness as separate and unique individuals.

Far too often, we complex, imperfect human beings drag our distorted, fragmented selves into relationships with other partial beings. One incomplete person meets another incomplete person. And the two, each seeking a helpmate to fulfill his or her deepest unmet emotional needs, marry and create not bliss but chaos. Unless help is sought to unravel the mess, the relationship is in serious trouble.

I turn to the portrait of the half woman once again, saddened by her pain and the loss of never having been completed. I think about the many men and women who face this same dilemma today, and I hope their portraits won't turn out like this one. As I walk away I feel a firm but reassuring hand on my shoulder. Without a word, Kansas acknowledges my sorrow and leads me into yet another discovery.

The Way We Are

My next find in the dungeonous chamber of past experiences is a box decorated in pretty rose-colored ribbons and paper, now faded with age. Curious as to its contents, I shake it. Nothing.

"Go ahead," Kansas says. "You can open it."

So I do. "There's another package," I exclaim with the enthusiasm of a child at Christmas. As I make my way through layer after layer of paper, tape, and ribbon, I finally come down to a small, gray, crusty blob. "Oh, fiddle," I burst out, disappointed at my find. It's just a rock. I toss it to the stone floor and it fractures. The beam of my flashlight reveals bouncing rainbow reflections of crystal. Gently I gather the broken treasure in my hands. "Beautiful," I murmur. "But why was it disguised so thoroughly? Why all the wrappings? What does it mean?"

"I suspect," says Kansas, "it's a picture of the way we are."

"I see." And I do. The rock, like so many of us, isn't really what it seemed to be. On the outside, the packaging made it seem big and brightly colored, when it was really only covered in layers and layers of false perceptions. Once I reached the object, I found a hard, rough surface. It wasn't until the shell was broken that I could see its delicate, crystalline interior.

The Tragic Loss of Self

The crystal represents the clear, pure center of who we were in the beginning, when God created man and woman in His perfect image. Before sin covered their crystalline core, Adam and Eve saw in themselves a reflection of God. He affirmed them and loved them and entrusted His creation to them.

Can you imagine what it must have been like—this warm, intimate relationship with God? What a privilege to be the only one of God's creations to be so bonded to the creator that He would call us His children! There were no identity problems, no loss of self-esteem, no sense of inadequacy—only truth and the reality of a loving God.

Then came Satan's seduction and sin. If the crystal represents our pure, true center, that which was created in God's image, then the stone's crusty, coarse outer parameters represent our shame-based self, the one we set up, much like Adam's fig leaf, in order to hide from God.

In studying and clarifying the concept of the lost self, I found the ideas of William Kirwan to be very helpful:

> When Adam and Eve fell, they lost their harmonious relationship with God, with the rest of creation, with one another, and even with their real selves. . . . When Adam told God that he hid because he was afraid, he was saying in essence, "I have lost God, so I no longer belong. I am afraid and insecure." He was also saying, "I have lost perfection, so I no longer feel a sense of self-esteem. Instead I feel guilty and ashamed." God asked Adam, "Who told you that you were naked?" Of course, no one had. God was accentuating the fact that the shame Adam felt was self-caused. Adam brought it on himself, and he was feeling its consequences. Finally, Adam was saying, "I have lost control, so I am weak and feel depressed." Before the fall, Adam was . . . strong enough to deal satisfactorily with any situation that might come his way . . . [meaning he was strong enough to resist *all* temptation, even the desire to be equal to God]. Now he no longer had that strength. He undoubtedly felt inferior and insignificant.[2]

In the fall Adam and Eve lost their sense of belonging—their identity, their innocence. Enveloped by sin, they could no longer see themselves with the clarity of God's viewpoint. All they had was their own faulty perception—and a self that was no longer whole and perfect as God had intended. Their true identity was covered and replaced by one of their own making.

Loss of identity, then, means being disconnected from God. And the situation is complicated by the legacy of inadequacy, rejection, shame, and helplessness that we carry in every part of our lives and pass on from generation to generation. Perhaps the most tragic aspect of all this loss is seen in the lives of the children. Unlike Adam and Eve, we don't start out in paradise. Our lives begin in a sinful environment, with imperfect parents in an imperfect world. From the beginning, then, we learn to see ourselves through that faulty perception rather than from God's point of view.

Most personality theorists agree that our identities are formed largely by how other people see us. If we see love and acceptance reflected in another person's eyes, we will tend to see ourselves as lovable and acceptable individuals. If we see anger and criticism in their eyes, we may come to see ourselves as unworthy and unacceptable.

As many of us grew up, we were told that we were bad if we became angry, or that we were babies if we cried. We were taught that only the weak allowed themselves to be emotional, and so we learned to stifle our feelings. And we may have discovered early on that we shouldn't be scared, or hurt, or upset—even when we were. Some of us were left to our own devices by parents who didn't care or have time. So we grew up feeling that we weren't worth bothering with. We may have learned not to trust who we are or what we feel because grown-ups were too big to argue with and they were always right.

We've come to be more accepting of emotions since I was a child, but many parents are still dictating what they want their children to become. Today we're more likely to see parents push their children toward high achievements. Some begin training while baby is still in utero, and daycare centers offer lessons in music and gymnastics. Baby has no choice, for the first few years anyway, but to adjust.

A child's defense to such pressures may well be to create a self that is acceptable to the world, created in the image of those around him. But inside hides a delicate self, a true identity which becomes lost under all the layers of the newly created false self.

Soul-Murder

John Bradshaw claims that the crisis in families today arises in part out of a lack of wholeness or "holiness," and that this lack is largely caused by shame and loss of the private self (the self created in the image of God).

Sometimes, in our inadequate attempts to discipline and set limits on children (which to some degree, of course, is necessary), families and societies overstep the boundaries and force the children to deny who they are and what they feel. Bradshaw says that, "to have one's feelings, body, desires and thoughts controlled is to lose one's self. To lose one's self is to have one's soul murdered."[3]

Eventually, as children grow up, the "real," healthy self—the unique God-created image—may be totally hidden by the many layers which form the "public" self. Sadly, we grow up without ever knowing who we really are. We then go through life equipped only with faulty perceptions of who and what we are. We may fall into compulsive and/or addictive behavior patterns in an attempt to cover up the shame and the loss of not being our real selves.

At this point, some of you may be feeling guilty over how you reared your own children. Others may be feeling angry over the way you were raised. I would suggest that you set aside those feelings for now. You may, at some point, want to seek counseling to help you deal with the feelings. But no matter how hard you try, you can't erase past events. You can't go back and rear your children again, nor can you alter the way your parents treated you. All you can do at this point is seek understanding and forgiveness and try to avoid repeating past mistakes.

I would also remind parents that no matter how wonderful you are or try to be as a parent, you will probably make mistakes. The purpose in all of this is not to take or lay blame, but rather to promote understanding and to enable you and your children to become the persons you were created to be.

The loss of the true self can undermine and destroy relationships without our even being aware of the problem. Perhaps what men and women need, then, is an opportunity to explore the deep, hidden chambers of their minds and souls so that the lost self can be found, cleansed, healed, and restored to wholeness (holiness).

Kansas is signaling that it's time to move on. I hate to leave this topic with so many things left unsaid, without resolution. But as Kansas reminds me, we'll be looking at resolutions to this and many other problems in Part 3. Right now, then, let's move on to another discovery.

The Child Inside

In a dark and dusty corner of the Temple of Doomed Relationships, something catches my eye. It's a large nesting doll. My Norwegian grandmother once brought me one from the old country. I loved it! Inside the outer doll nestled a smaller doll, and inside her was another, then another—like mothers having babies generation after generation.

In wiping away some of the dust, I find the outer doll perfectly preserved. The paint is barely chipped.

I twist her open. Disappointment floods me. The inner doll is scarred; her once bright paint is dull and chipped.

As I pull this second doll apart, my heart sinks. I feel as though a fist has been jammed into my stomach. The tiny doll inside is shattered.

"How could this happen?" I cry to no one in particular. "How could the outside doll be so perfect while the inside has fallen apart?"

"That," says Kansas with a wisdom I've come to admire, "is the symbol of the wounded child who lives inside of us."

Like me, you probably consider yourself a mature, well-adjusted adult. Yet have you ever had times when it suddenly dawned on you that you were acting like a child?

I was especially struck by this concept one day when my husband was sitting in his recliner. "Honey," I said, "I need a couple of bucks. Do you have it, or shall I go to the cash machine?"

He frowned and said, "What do you need money for now? You just went to the store yesterday. You're going to bankrupt us . . ." Well, you get the picture. Once Ron gets into his Frugal Fred routine, there's no stopping him.

As he muttered about this expense and that expense, I found my muscles tightening. I drew my hands into fists and stomped off like an adolescent. "Forget I asked! I was just going to pick up some milk, for Pete's sake!"

Suddenly a picture from my junior-high days flashed into my mind. My family didn't have much money when I was a kid. As I mentioned before, my father was often too ill to work, and we lived on a pension. I can remember him sitting up in his bed, thin and frail. My two younger brothers and I would come in to see him before school to say good-bye and to ask for three cents apiece for milk money. Probably not every day, but often enough to feel like every day, he would lecture us on the value of money. It used to make me furious that he'd have such a fit over three lousy pennies.

As an adult, I can look back and understand how he must have felt—clutching for even a semblance of control in a life that, more often than not, seemed to be slipping out of his grasp. But I was a child who didn't understand his concern, his losses and needs. All I felt at the time was that he cared more about money than about me.

Ron's response to me triggered a reaction from an angry child within whose real problem was not lack of money but more likely anger toward an absent father.

All of us struggle to some degree with childhood memories, whether conscious or unconscious, that cause us to react in certain ways. The past can play an intricate part in who we are and how we see ourselves, as well as how we relate to others.

In establishing what men and women need in one another, it may be helpful to gain a sense of the child within us who, whether we like it or not, is part of the relationship. Sometimes problems involving a wounded inner child can be handled simply by knowing the cause. Other times the trauma may be deep and painful enough to require a therapist who is experienced in inner healing.

"We'd better be heading out if we want to reach the yacht by nightfall," Kansas says as he holds open the door and glances at his watch.

I must admit I'm more than ready to go. Exploring the inner recesses of the Temple of Doomed Relationships has dug up a lot of relics for me to think about. How about you?

- Have you discovered or sensed the possibility of a wounded child inside of you?
- Is there, somewhere deep within your soul, a lost self who longs to live the kind of life God intended you to live?
- Have you been struggling to build up self-esteem in an image—a false self—that was created to cover your real identity as a human being created in God's image?
- Are you living the kind of existence you really want to live?
- Are you still trying to change people to fit into the role you want them to play?
- Are you trying to make yourself fit into a mold you see as ideal?

These are some valid points to consider as we follow Kansas up the steep stairway and into the light to prepare for our journey back to the *Kristiana*. As we chug downstream toward the sea, I think how far we've come since our imaginary cruise began. In the Fantasy Islands we dreamed of perfect mates and dared to make wishes. As we maneuvered through Reality Straits, we discovered the truth about fairy tales and exposed the demons that destroy relationships. We examined the detrimental effects of dysfunctional family systems; lack of wholeness; loss of self; the inner wounded child; divorce, affairs, and lust; wanting and making changes; and unrealistic expectations.

The jungle and its temple ruins are behind us now, and in a few minutes we'll climb back aboard the *Kristiana*. By tomorrow's sunrise we'll be leaving Reality's exposed and troubled terrain, taking with us only memories as souvenirs of the revealing journey. Some of your memories may be hurtful ones—digging up the past can bring pain as well as understanding. But when you can pinpoint the problems in an unhappy and failing relationship, you've made the first step toward finding a solution.

As our tour boat nears the mouth of the river, we see the *Kristiana* anchored offshore, awaiting our return. The sea is choppy, making our access to the yacht a laborious one. The skies overhead are dark and ominous, filled with a threat of rain.

"I'll be leaving you," Kansas declares as we approach the *Kristiana*, "just as soon as I take care of the boat and check in with David."

"Leaving? You mean for good? You won't be here to guide us anymore?" I ask, suddenly feeling a little like the rain clouds above us. I've come to like Kansas and his eccentric ways.

"I have some reconciling of my own to do," he says in a voice strangely strained. "God knows I waited long enough."

"I hope it goes well," I tell him sincerely as we leave him in the boat and climb aboard our mother vessel, ". . . and thanks."

I am midway up the ladder when the thought hits me. "Kansas, wait! You can't leave yet. David's gone! Who's going to run the boat?"

An hour later, an obviously disappointed Kansas stands at the helm and expertly eases the yacht through the narrow straits and into open water. I'm beside him, feeling a little guilty. But as my gaze sweeps across the sky, I can see a silver lining at the end of the storm front. Sunshine and clouds, tears and rainbows, despair and hope—that's reality. And it is hope we will give our thoughts to as we trim our sails and let the wind carry us to the soothing, healing waters of Reconciliation Bay.

Part III
Reconciliation Bay

I T ' S   M I D D A Y when we drop anchor in Reconciliation Bay. The sun is playing peekaboo with fluffy white cotton balls floating in a cornflower blue sky. Relaxing in our lounge chairs on deck, we watch the clouds turn to unicorns, dragons, castles, and people with strange and ever-changing shapes and sizes.

I take a sip from a tall, frosty glass of limeade and direct my attention to Kansas as he eases the *Kristiana* between coral-reef shelves. Kansas, as you might recall, was set to leave us after our tour into Reality's jungle. But just as he was ready to leave, I told him David had gone, so he was forced to give up his plans.

I'm glad Kansas is staying, even though he doesn't seem all that happy about it. But he needs the quietness of this place—we all do, after struggling through the perils of Reality Straits. It's too bad David isn't here to experience Reconciliation Bay with us. But maybe he can still come to reconciliation in his own way and in his own time.

Fantasy had its glass slippers and ideal mates, Reality had its dragons and jungles, but Reconciliation? Ah, yes. Reconciliation Bay has golden sandy beaches scattered generously with shells of every variety. Off the reefs, bright fish flash in the blue-green water, beckoning us to explore the bay's secrets and bathe in its sparkling clear depths.

The waves roll in and break lazily on the shore. On land, a wide expanse of sand is bordered by tropical plants and trees on one side and a sloping hill on the other. The hill looks like a patchwork quilt with its grassy, emerald-green slopes and charcoal rock. A structure at the top catches my eye.

"Look—on the top of the hill. What is it?"

"That would be the Sanctuary," Kansas says. "Our home for the next few days."

"Really," I respond, suddenly eager to go ashore. "It looks like a perfect place to rest."

"Yes, ma'am," Kansas drawls, "and to get in touch with God."

In the next four chapters we'll get to the heart of what men and women need most in each other. And we will learn how and by whom those needs can be met as we find harmony in our relationship to God, to ourselves, and to others.

Now let's explore this peaceful place. I'm told it promises rare gifts of solitude and contentment to those who ask.

Chapter 11
Reconciling With God

SAMANTHA LEANED AGAINST the ship's railing and stared into the transparent aquamarine water, watching a black and yellow fish with a sliver of a nose dart back and forth and upside down, as if he had no purpose, no sense of direction. He looked like she felt. They had sailed from Reality Straits four days ago, and David still hadn't come back.

"What happens now?" Kansas asked, sauntering across the deck to join her.

"What? Oh . . . well, I guess it's time to disembark and lead our guests up to the Sanctuary."

"I didn't mean with them. I meant with you and David."

"Nothing . . . apparently." Sam lifted her head and took a deep breath. She didn't want to talk about David. She didn't want to cry anymore, and if Kansas turned his compassion on her, she'd do just that. "He's not coming back, so I guess it's over. I'd rather not discuss it anymore."

"Look, Sam, I know it's none of my business, but . . ."

"You're right. It isn't."

Kansas cleared his throat, unwilling to leave it alone. He knew

David too well to believe the man would just walk out of a relationship. "Don't you think you should try to contact him?"

"No! And don't you, either. I was a fool to think I could trust him—or any man. You can bet I'll never make that mistake again."

"Bitterness doesn't suit you, Samantha."

"What would you know about it? You've never . . ."

"Never what? Lost a lover? Been abandoned? Abused?" Kansas closed his eyes and shielded them with his hand. He didn't want to talk about it—the memories hurt too much. But maybe his experience could help Sam work through hers. He took a deep breath to clear away the heaviness those memories always brought, covered her hand with his own, and began, "I know, Sam—believe me, I know. My mother used to beat my brother and me with a razor strap and lock us in the closet for hours at a time. She disappeared when I was five, and I remember my dad saying, 'You boys have really done it this time.' I was certain whatever happened had been my fault. It wasn't until I grew up that I learned she'd been committed to a mental hospital. I found out about it because she had committed suicide and the authorities had to notify her next of kin."

"Oh, Kansas, I'm so sorry."

"I grew up hating her for leaving us and hating myself for making her leave. I hated my dad, too, because even though he took care of our physical needs, he never once held us or said, 'I love you.' I kept seeing visions of that little boy curled up in the dark, sobbing, and nobody came, nobody cared."

"That's awful."

"Yes, it was." Kansas took a long deep breath and exhaled slowly. "But the point is, Sam, I don't hate them anymore. I spent twenty years of my life being angry and distrustful—I thought I was being tough. I had a hard time relating to women, and deep down I resented them. But I also needed a woman to give me the love my mother never could. After college I married Jill. She was the sweetest, most sensitive woman I'd ever met.

One day, not long after our wedding, we had an argument over something—I don't remember what. And I got so mad, I . . . I hit her."

Sam stared at him, wanting to argue that the Kansas she knew was too kind—too understanding—for that kind of violence. But the pain in his eyes told her that every word he'd said was true.

Kansas raked his fingers through his hair and continued, his voice raw with emotion. "I'll never forget the look in her eyes. The hurt, the terror." He shook his head and focused on a piece of driftwood on the beach. "I panicked and took off. I couldn't believe that rage had come out of me. I had totally lost control. I was afraid I'd gone crazy like my mother."

"What happened to Jill?"

He hesitated and frowned. "I don't know. That's something I hope to find out on my next trip home. I think I'm ready to face her now. I need to ask her to forgive me."

"And you?" Sam asked. "You're not angry anymore."

Kansas smiled. "I tried a lot of self-improvement stuff on how to control my temper, how to relate to people. I even saw a counselor a couple of times. I'm sure it all helped, but not enough. A few years ago, I stopped running and . . . well, I ended up here."

"In Reconciliation Bay?"

He nodded. "I rested, Samantha, and I listened. I met the risen Christ and made my peace with God."

"And you think I should, too."

Kansas shrugged his shoulders. "It sure beats letting hate and resentment tear you apart."

"Nothing is tearing me apart. The way I figure it, God dealt me a lousy hand when I came into this world. I finally decided that the only way I was going to survive in life was to start drawing a few aces. I did that . . . by myself. I didn't need anybody's help then, and I still don't."

Samantha moved away from Kansas. "Looks like it's time for

us to go ashore," she said as the lifeboat snuggled against the *Kristiana* and waited to haul the rest of her crew to land.

As Samantha started to leave, Kansas touched her arm. She turned back to face him. "So, you chose a fistful of aces. Good for you. But Sam, think a minute. Who do you think made those aces available to you?"

Sam frowned and shook her head. "I suppose you're going to tell me God did."

Kansas smiled and draped an arm around her shoulder. "I believe He did. You don't have to make any decisions right now. I know how hard it is to accept and trust in God when so many terrible things have happened to you. All I ask is that you open your heart and listen. Maybe spend some time with Michael—he's a priest and counselor who works here. Give yourself up to this place. Find out who God is and how He feels about you."

Sam sighed. It was hard to stay mad at a man like Kansas. He acted as if he really cared about her. "Okay, I'll listen. I'll try to keep an open mind."

"That's my girl. We'd better get a move on. Our guests are getting restless."

Maybe it was time, Samantha thought as she climbed into the lifeboat. Time to stop running—to stop the anger. At a very young age she'd taken control of her life. Lived it her own way. But since she had met David, she didn't know what her way was anymore. Logically, she should never have married him; the computer had only paired them because David had cheated. Yet in her heart, she still wanted him, longed to touch him and hold him. But no, she had to stop torturing herself with romantic thoughts of David. It was too late for her marriage, but maybe not for her. She'd listen, although she wasn't making any promises.

The ship is empty now. Samantha, Kansas, the crew and passengers are meandering up the path to the ancient, castlelike structure built into the side of the hill. The ship's radio squawks for attention, but no one hears.

"I'm sorry, ma'am," the ship-to-shore operator said in a crackly voice. "I can't raise anyone aboard the *Kristiana*."

"Thank you. I'll try again later." The woman quietly returned the receiver to its cradle so as not to wake her son. His normally suntanned face looked pale and drawn. She had been praying for him constantly since the ranch foreman had discovered him and Jennie at the bottom of the ravine. The horse had been killed, and she thanked God continually that it hadn't been the other way around.

"His chances are good," the doctor had said, "since he's so strong." And this morning he'd finally regained consciousness. It was his heart that worried her . . . that woman had broken his heart.

Her son was as tight-lipped as his father—rest his soul—and he hadn't told her why his honeymoon had been cut short. All she knew was that without so much as a fare-thee-well, David had taken a wife and then come home without her. But Mary Jo Hartley knew heartache when she saw it, and the raw pain of it tore her apart every time she looked into her son's eyes.

"O-o-o-h." David heard a groan, then realized it had come from him. He'd come to hate these slips into consciousness. With wakefulness came the throbbing pain. He turned his head to the side, sensing his mother's presence. "Hi," David croaked. It hurt to talk. It even hurt to breathe. He vaguely remembered things he had been told in brief interludes of consciousness. A punctured lung. Right leg broken in two places. Concussion.

At least you're alive, he reminded himself. He also remembered that the last time he'd opened his eyes it was to learn he had been unconscious for three days and Jennie hadn't made it. He might as well have died, too, for all the good living was doing him now. He was forced to lie there, helpless, while Samantha slipped further and further from his grasp. If only he could talk with her, maybe . . .

"Samantha . . ." David tried to raise himself, but the movement sharpened the ache in his chest and he abandoned the idea.

"Did you . . ." he made no effort to finish.

"I placed a call with the ship-to-shore operator, but there was no response."

"I've got to . . ." He tried to move again, driven by his need to reach Samantha.

"I know. Please lie still, David. Try not to get upset. I'll keep trying."

But David knew that once the party had gone ashore there would be no way to reach her. Reconciliation Bay had no telephones; it wasn't even on the map. Hope drained from him as quickly as his strength. He sank back into the pillows and let his mother wipe the perspiration from his face. Giving himself up to the pain, David prayed for the blessed release that could only come through death.

"How Could You Have Let This Happen?"

Samantha and David have given up hope of ever getting back together. But I haven't, and it appears that Kansas hasn't either.

"How could you have let this happen?" Kansas says to me as he drops back from the others and walks with me up the hill.

"What?" Winded from the long climb, I stop to catch my breath.

"Samantha and David are right for each other. You're the writer; do something."

I don't answer. Why indeed? I created them—Samantha, David, Kansas, and the others—out of my imagination and from the experiences of people I know. Yet they seem to have taken on a life of their own.

Why did David take that fall with his horse? Why did Samantha and Kansas have to come out of such painful childhoods? Why are David's and Samantha's hearts breaking with the knowledge that their relationship is over? Who knows why bad things happen—even to fictional characters.

And with that my thoughts turn to God. God designed into us the power to choose between good and evil. This power to choose is at the same time a wonderful and awful freedom because we all too often make the wrong decisions. So much of what God does, I imagine, is to pick up the pieces of our shattered lives that come as a result of wrong choices and to help us straighten up the messes we create for ourselves and for others.

Sadly, God is rarely credited with the good He works out of our human failures. Instead He is blamed for all our troubles. I've often heard people say things like, "How could God take my husband away?" or "I could never believe in a God who would allow a child to be abused."

I certainly understand. I too have gone to God, just as Kansas came to me, and said, "God, how could You let this happen?" I particularly remember one incident that happened when I was a nurse. I was caring for a baby with a terminal disease. Little Andy could not cry or move or even open his eyes. For three weeks we cared for him, held him, fed him, and grew to love him. Then one night Andy died in my arms. In the car on the way home, I spilled out my grief and anger to God. "Why?" I cried. "What did this innocent baby ever do to deserve this?"

It's a question we all struggle with from time to time. And I still don't fully understand why terrible things happen. I believe that in part our troubles come because we live in a fallen world and we are subject to its diseases and its disasters. In part we are punished for our sins. But there is also suffering we can't account for, things we simply don't understand.

Whatever the reason for our pain and suffering, I have learned enough about God to trust Him completely and know that He wants what's best for those who love Him. And I know whatever happens, for whatever reason, I must be content to acknowledge my limited view and trust that God sees the whole picture as well as the final outcome. But believing in God and trusting Him to meet our needs isn't always easy for us, especially when far too many disappointments obliterate our childlike trust in a God we can't see.

"What happened to David?" Kansas asks, interrupting my philosophical thoughts.

I frown. "I can't tell you that, Kansas. It's not for you to know yet. In time you'll learn all the secrets, but for now you'll have to work with what you have."

"Well, at least give me some time with Samantha," he says. "Make her listen."

"You'll have the time. Love has made her vulnerable— softened her heart. Her anger and bitterness are only a cover-up for the hurt she doesn't want anyone to see. But you know as well as I do that in the final chapter, she will have to make her own choices as to whether or not to listen or act on what you've said."

Kansas nods. "I know. I've been there."

We enter the courtyard and fall into the awed silence the place seems to require of us. Bottlebrush plants and birds of paradise—a myriad of colorful blossoms—border a large expanse of lawn. An ornate fountain adorns the cobbled walk leading to a turreted stone structure draped with clumps of ivy and topped with a steep slate roof.

In His Sanctuary

Kansas grasps the black wrought-iron handle of the massive wooden door and beckons me inside. The room is furnished sparsely. High-backed wooden benches line the walls. A balcony juts out from the side and back walls, and beyond it I can see our individual rooms.

The wooden floor is parted in the center by a blue carpet that ends at a long kneeling rail. Beyond that stands an altar, above it a cross extending nearly to the top of the two-story, vaulted ceiling. On one side of the cross, light streams through a stained-glass portrait of the Shepherd Christ, and on the other, the dying Christ of the Crucifixion.

Elegant. Moving. And the simple truth of it jolts my senses. I have visited temples and churches and been awed by their artistic and aesthetic beauty. Yet here, in this place, it isn't the building or the glass or even the cross that inspires me. Here, in the sanctuary of my heart, in the depths of my soul, I stand in the Presence of God.

And it is into that Presence that each of us must come with our broken hearts, with our wounded spirits, and with our disintegrating relationships in order to find true and lasting peace of mind. It is here—in humility, openness, and oneness with the Creator—that healing can be found. This is what men and women need before they can even begin to consider what they need in one another.

Kansas nudges me to let me know that, while I can return here anytime I want, there is still more to see before this chapter ends. We walk through a door at the far left-hand corner of the Sanctuary.

Learn of Him

"A library," I say, pleased to think I can spend some time reading and studying.

"This isn't an ordinary library," Kansas says. "It's filled with Bibles and commentaries, dictionaries and lexicons. There are classics from the desert fathers, Martin Luther, St. John of the Cross, Andrew Murray. They're all here—the famous priests, monks, saints, and people of God who changed the world. Here you can learn as much as you want about God."

Since we are in the library, this might be a good opportunity to clarify what it means to be reconciled to God.

The concept of God's being reconciled to humankind—that is, of His being in intimate relationship with us—doesn't seem to exist in pagan religions. The Bible tells us:

185

It was the Father's good pleasure for all the fulness to dwell in Him, and through Him to reconcile all things to Himself, having made peace through the blood of His cross; through Him, I say, whether things on earth or things in heaven. And although you were formerly alienated and hostile in mind, engaged in evil deeds, yet He has now reconciled you in His fleshly body through death, in order to present you before Him holy and blameless and beyond reproach (Colossians 1:19–21).

Through His death on the Cross, Christ removed all obstacles between the created and the Creator. In a sense, the phrase "He reconciled" sums up the Gospel message for us. In two words, the apostle Paul tells us that Christ removed the barriers that kept us from being one with God. The impact of reconciliation can be seen in light of the cost. One need only read the account of Christ's journey to the Cross and imagine the terrible agony— both emotional and physical—that He suffered on our account.

Even though the act of reconciliation was done once and for all, each of us has a choice as to whether or not we want to accept it. The Bible tells us we can be:

- reconciled with God, being holy and blameless, looking forward to eternal life, or we can . . .
- remain a stranger, an enemy to God, being in alliance with Satan, wicked, hostile—doomed to eternal death.

The message of reconciliation is an invitation that asks us to join the living God. An RSVP is required and we are accepted by saying yes to God.

Kansas and I slip silently out of the library and close the door, understanding how important this place is to knowing God.

Seek Solitude

As we are reconciled with God we will want to take time daily to be with Him, gradually coming to understand the depth of the

Father's love for us, His beloved children. But how can we know God in such an intimate way? What can we do to find inner peace and healing? Study, of course, gives us answers in part, but knowledge won't necessarily fill the needs of the soul. Perhaps another part of the answer can be found in the silence of the secluded room that waits for each of us at the upper level.

I walk into my room alone and am reminded that coming to know God is an intimate, private affair. I can listen to others, read books, but in the end, if I am to make Him part of my life, I must come to Him alone and let His Spirit enter me.

The room is sparse and bare, with only a washbasin, a cot, and a small lamp for reading. And it is with this kind of simplicity and bareness of heart, mind, and soul that I must approach God.

Solitude with its blissful silence doesn't always have to be found in a room like this, isolated from others (although those moments when no one is around are times to be treasured). Solitude can also be a place in the heart which we can visit at any time, anywhere. Through the psalmist, God says, "Cease striving and know that I am God" (Psalms 46:10).

Silence used to make me feel uncomfortable, but not anymore. As my world spins noisily and crazily on its axis and the work-to-be-done list grows faster than I can keep up with it, I welcome the silence—my special quiet time with God.

What is it like to be intimate with God? I have found it is like:

- joining with One whose love for me means more than life itself.
- being a child and lying in the arms of a loving Father who would never leave or forsake me.
- finding a quiet place within my heart to listen for the still, small voice of God.
- being a centered ball of clay—at one with the Master who forms me.
- being satisfied—with every need fulfilled.

A Matter of Needs

I have been in my room for some time now, considering my need for God, when I become aware of a more elemental need—food. I wander down the hall to look for Kansas and find him leaning against an ornately carved beam on the balcony.

"I'm hungry," I say. "When's lunch?"

He smiles and with a gentleness I haven't seen in him before says, "We won't be eating meals today. There's food in the kitchen if you want it, but you might want to join me in fasting and partaking only of spiritual food."

"Hmmm," I say thoughtfully, remembering Jesus' words from the Sermon on the Mount. " 'Blessed are those who hunger and thirst for righteousness, for they shall be satisfied' " (Matthew 5:6).

Kansas nods. "Have you ever wondered what our lives might be like if every day, before even considering our needs and wants, we first came into the Presence of God and ate of the Bread of Life and drank of His Living Water? I'll bet our need list would shrink dramatically."

I agree.

The theory that we must have our elemental needs for food, water, and shelter met before we can consider spiritual things has become widely accepted in our culture. Abraham Maslow, who popularized this particular "hierarchy of needs," has quite a reputation among psychologists even today. And, of course, there's a lot of truth in the idea. Physically, we would die without food and water. And if you were lost in an Alaskan snowstorm, you'd turn into a popsicle without clothes and a place to come in from the cold.

But God didn't create us in a purely physical form. We are body, mind, and spirit. And if I were to list my own hierarchy of needs, the first item on my list would be reconciliation to and intimacy with God.

I believe this is especially valid as we examine this matter of male-female relationships. What men and women need most in one another is for each of them as separate and unique individuals to become one with the God who created them.

Why would I come to this outrageous conclusion? It must have been something Jesus said:

> . . . Do not be anxious for your life, as to what you shall eat, or what you shall drink; nor for your body, as to what you shall put on. Is not life more than food, and the body than clothing? Look at the birds of the air, that they do not sow, neither do they reap, nor gather into barns, and yet your heavenly Father feeds them. Are you not worth much more than they? . . . And why are you anxious about clothing? Observe how the lilies of the field grow; they do not toil nor do they spin, yet I say to you that even Solomon in all his glory did not clothe himself like one of these. But if God so arrays the grass of the field, which is alive today and tomorrow is thrown into the furnace, will He not much more do so for you, O men [women] of little faith? Do not be anxious then, saying, "What shall we eat?" or "What shall we drink?" or "With what shall we clothe ourselves?" For all these things the Gentiles [ungodly] eagerly seek; for your heavenly Father knows that you need all these things. *But seek first His kingdom and His righteousness; and all these things shall be added to you* (Matthew 6:25–34, emphasis added).

Jesus went to great lengths to reassure us that our basic physical needs would be provided for if we placed ourselves in God's hands. God has given us the earth as a resource, and by working, using our brains, pooling our talents, and caring for one another, our physical needs can be for the most part taken care of.

Yet all too often we find ourselves confusing our wants and needs. We struggle to get rather than to give. We want, we need, and we ache to be fulfilled. But we can have our physical needs met until pineapples grow wild in the Antarctic and still be unsatisfied. Maybe we're hungry because we have our priorities turned around!

If-Only People

I can't help but think about people who have everything they could want and still hunger for more. These are the "if only" people. I used to be one. I guess, if I were to be truly honest, I'd have to admit that I still am one at times when I lose sight of what is really important. I used to think that happiness and satisfaction lay just around the corner. The "if onlys" started early in my life and I carried them on into adulthood. I could be happy, I thought, if only . . .

- I could stay out as late as I wanted to . . .
- I were an adult . . .
- I could get a date with Jim . . . Ted . . . John . . . Ron . . .
- I had my very own cherry-red Thunderbird convertible . . .
- I had a college education . . .
- I had a lot of money . . .
- I could travel around the world . . .
- I could get married . . .
- I hadn't gotten married . . .
- I had a mansion overlooking the ocean . . .
- I had children . . .
- my children would leave home . . .
- I could run away from home . . .

Have you ever watched a cow or horse strain against a fence (even if it's barbed wire) to grab a mouthful of the grass on the other side? We laugh at their foolishness, knowing the grass is equally dispersed on either side. Yet nearly all of us have strained against our personal fences, longing to get a taste of life on the other side.

I'd still like to own a house overlooking the ocean! But I know now that no material thing I collect, no person I fill my life with, can satisfy the needs of my soul. It seems that the more we experience, the more we own and collect, the deeper and more pronounced and more demanding the soul hunger becomes. For what, indeed, does it profit a person to gain the world and lose his or her soul? (See Mark 8:36.)

The End Is Only the Beginning

My thoughts on needs had taken me out of the Sanctuary, and I found myself sitting on a stone bench overlooking the bay. I become aware of footsteps crunching on a graveled path. "Thought you might like to see this," Kansas says as he comes to sit beside me. In his hand he carries a book entitled *His Life Is Mine.*

I am familiar with the volume. The author, Archimandrite Sophrany, was born in 1896, in Czarist Russia, to Orthodox parents. He searched for and found his peace with God through contemplation, prayer, and spiritual oneness. He came to God as a lover of nature, an artist, a theologian, and he devoted his last twenty-some years to God as a monk, sharing his knowledge and understanding with others.

"Look," Kansas says, pointing to a highlighted text. "This relates to what you've been saying about reconciliation to God being our highest need. Listen to what the translator says about him in the introduction":

Daily life [for Sophrany] now flowed on the periphery, as it were, of external events. The one thing needful was to discover the purport of our appearance on this planet; to revert to the moment before creation and to be merged with our original source. [Sophrany was] utterly preoccupied by the thought that if man died without the possibility of returning to the sphere of Absolute Being, then life held no meaning. [He believed that] civilization can only be as strong as the inner lives of its people.[1]

"That's so true," I tell Kansas. "And we can easily apply the principle to marriage, because a relationship is only as strong as the inner, spiritual lives of the two who form it."

"I've often wondered what my marriage to Jill might have been like if I'd known then what I know now. I just wish . . ." Kansas begins, then quickly changes the subject. "You know, what I liked best about this Sophrany guy was the way he saw God's presence manifested in everything. He was . . ." Kansas turns back to the book and reads: " '. . . full to the brim with awareness of God.'[2] I like that." He looks up and adds, "When that fullness comes, it's like you don't need anything else . . . it's as though you're complete . . . and satisfied."

"That's beautiful, Kansas," I agree, deciding not to push him on his abrupt switch of topics. I know his wish involves reconciliation with Jill. I want the best for Kansas, so maybe before this book is over I'll try to figure out a way to make his wish come true.

We've come to the end of our chapter on reconciliation with God, yet in a very real sense it is only the beginning. For me, the answers to a satisfying life lie not in having my wants and desires fulfilled (although, I have to admit, I feel doubly blessed when they are) but in being one with God.

Study and pray. Find a place of solitude and meditate. For what men and women really need is to know God intimately so that in time we can all be brimming with His Presence.

Sunsets are like splashes of color on an artist's canvas in Reconciliation Bay. Samantha has come out to view one of God's most fantastic scenes with us. "It's really beautiful here," she muses, her tone wistful. "I'm glad we came."

We agree, then fall into silence, allowing the sky to shout, sing, and whisper its own resplendent tribute to its Creator. On the way back to the Sanctuary for a much-needed sleep, I hear Samantha whisper to Kansas, "Ah . . . I need to talk to you."

Kansas glances around. "Well, everyone else has gone in; I guess this is as good a time as any."

"I . . . ah . . . look, I'm sorry for being so rude to you this morning."

Kansas nods. "You were upset."

"Yeah, I . . . well, as much as I hate to admit it, you were right. I took your advice and talked to that counselor—Michael—today. I talked to God, too."

"Did you?"

"Yes, and I believe now. I've accepted Christ as my Savior."

His arm encircles her shoulder and he pulls her to him in a warm embrace. "I'm glad."

"I made an appointment to talk to Michael some more tomorrow. He works here; he says he'll help me resolve some of my conflicts and work on what he called my 'faulty belief system.' "

"Then you'd best get a good night's sleep. You've got a long day ahead."

We would all do well to take his advice. Our tomorrow could be as exhausting as Samantha's. So let's turn in—then on to the next chapter, where we'll discover what we can do to be reconciled to the person God created us to be. There, as we search for seashells and stroll along the beach, we'll learn how to enter a relationship as whole men and women who no longer need what another half person can't give them.

Chapter 12
Reconciling to Self

WHILE SAMANTHA WAS sleeping peacefully in the Sanctuary at Reconciliation Bay, David was growling at everyone who came near him.

"Son," Mary Jo Hartley said in her stern, no-nonsense style, "stop acting like a two-year-old with a temper tantrum. You're a grown man, and it's time you put that temper aside and settle down."

"Two-year-old?" David would have laughed if it didn't hurt so much. "I'm sorry. It's just so darned hard to lie here when I've got so much . . ."

"You've got no choice," his mother said flatly as she picked up her knitting. "Why don't you tell me what's troubling you? Might help to talk it out."

"Talking isn't going to get me back to Samantha. I've got to get out of this bed." He didn't try this time; his futile attempts at walking out of the place had left him with enough pain to last a lifetime.

"Honestly, you're just like your father used to be. Stubborn as all get out." Mary Jo sighed and rested her knitting on her lap. "I thought I taught you better."

194

"What do you mean? I'm not like him. I wish I were. He would never have gotten himself into this situation."

"You still see your father as some kind of hero, don't you?"

"Well, he was."

"In some ways, I suppose that's true. But he was also a man with many faults."

"I suppose no one is perfect. But I bet he came close."

"David, I loved your father very much, but I can't let you go on berating yourself because you can't measure up to the image you've created of him."

"He was a good father," David said, remembering with affection the giant of a man who'd taught him how to ride and shoot.

"Yes, but you were quick to learn, and so eager to please him. Sometimes I wonder if you aren't still trying to please him. He was a very impatient man. He vented his anger on anyone who stood in the way of what he wanted. Your father wasn't the kind of man who could admit his mistakes—whatever happened was always someone else's fault. He maintained a rigid control over everything he owned, me included. I wouldn't have minded that so much except that he never seemed able to talk to me about the things that really mattered. Do you know he never told me he loved me? We nearly lost the ranch two different times, and I never knew until he died. John had no tolerance for what he saw as weakness, especially not in himself—that's where you and he are alike. You seem to have a great deal of trouble accepting your weakness. You put on a great front. All those feelings churning around inside you, and all you've managed to show is your impatience."

David didn't speak. What his mother had said wasn't exactly true. He had opened up to Samantha, and look where it had gotten him. Numbness settled over him as he tried to fit the bits and pieces of information about his father into the picture of the man he thought he had known so well.

"Anyway, instead of talking over problems and concerns with

195

me, he'd leave home for a few days, drink himself silly and . . ."
Mary Jo hesitated. The memories dug painfully into her heart,
and she drew a ragged breath. "Your father didn't die a hero,
David." David watched his mother's lips quiver and tighten.
"He had been drinking heavily the night he died. He wasn't
speeding to get that woman in his car to a hospital. David, your
father was having an affair. He drove over the cliff because he
was drunk. No one ever knew, except Sheriff Tucker and me,
what really happened that night."

David closed his eyes. "You should have told me."

"You were too young to understand . . . and it hurt too much.
I wanted you to remember the good things. Your father *was* a
hero, but he was also a very weak man."

Over the next few days, David's body made excellent progress
in its healing. The chest tube was removed, his headaches disappeared, and his leg was casted. His mind was another story.
The shocking news about his father had dredged up unpleasant
memories of his family life he had long ago pushed from consciousness. He had begun to see a lot of his father in himself—
the need for control, for having things his way.

Perhaps the worst part of it all was that David wasn't sure who
he was anymore. And the more he looked inside himself, the
more confused and discouraged he became. He'd be leaving the
hospital tomorrow, but then what? The only thing he knew for
certain was that he had to get back to Samantha. He'd been
wrong in so many ways. David struggled to hold on to the hope
that once he apologized to her she would be willing to give their
marriage another chance.

Doubts assailed him as another danger presented itself clearly
in his mind. Samantha was a beautiful woman, alone, vulnerable. What if she and Kansas. . . . No, he wouldn't think about
it. He trusted Kansas with his life. *Yes*, a voice inside him per-
sisted, *but can you trust him with your wife?*

David opened the bedside-table mirror to shave. He looked as
pale and weak as he felt. "Maybe that would be best," David

said to his mirrored image. "Kansas is a far better man than you'll ever be."

A Healthy Dose of Self-Esteem

What David needs right now is a healthy dose of self-esteem and a little perspective on reality. David's father wasn't perfect—let's face it, he was a louse. But in a way he was also a victim. He died trying to live up to a myth so many men in our society fall for.

"The male machine is a special kind of being, different from women, children, and men who don't measure up," says Marc Feigen Fasteau in his book, *The Male Machine*. The author goes on to describe details of the way such a mechanism functions:

- "He is functional, designed mainly for work.
- He is programmed to tackle jobs, override obstacles, attack problems, overcome difficulties, and always seize the offensive.
- He will take on any task that can be presented to him in a competitive framework, and his most important positive reinforcement is victory.
- He has armor plating which is virtually impregnable.
- His circuits are never scrambled or overrun by irrelevant personal signals.
- He dominates and outperforms his fellows, although without excessive flashing of lights or clashing gears.
- His relationships with other male machines is one of respect but not intimacy. . . .
- His internal circuitry is something of a mystery to him and is maintained primarily by humans of the opposite sex.
- These delightful creatures service him with love and devotion by recognition of his superior design and the importance of his functions.
- He wields his authority over them effortlessly and magnanimously. Attempts at insurrection are easily squashed by re-

197

minding the would-be rebels of the facts of life—a quick pulse from the warning light and a simple but awe-inspiring flex of mechanical muscle usually does the job—while he rewards the most loyal and beautiful of his servants with the fruits of his labor and sexual performances."[1]

This mechanical male is not real, of course, but rather an alter ego set in the minds of "nearly every man in America." A real, human male can't live up to the image. But as the author suggests, "It is the yardstick against which we measure ourselves as men. To the extent that we fail to meet its injunctions, even by deliberate choice, we are likely to see ourselves, at least at times, as inadequate."[2]

David and millions of other men like him are trying to live out this ideal male image and comparing their performance to that ideal. The result is a world full of men who feel they are inferior and don't measure up. Yet we rarely hear about these feelings of failure. Most men are masters at covering up their feelings.

Women today have pressed hard for men to become more open, vulnerable, intimate, and honest. With all that's been written on intimacy, men and their feelings, and effective methods of communication, you'd think the walls men build around themselves would quickly crumble, but they don't.

Are Women Really Being Honest?

Perhaps it's because women, even though they seem more willing to talk, to share feelings, and to express their wants and needs openly, also have an image to live up to. Women tend to be more emotional than men, but are we really honest? Is what we openly say really what we feel inside? Perhaps both men and women fear the idea of showing too much of their true selves lest they be ridiculed, detested, deserted, or left lonely and unloved.

Perhaps we women have our own version of the Male Machine. Ours might be titled the Ultimate Woman or Supermom.

As a society we don't especially like to hear about people's weaknesses. We don't like to face our weaknesses, vulnerabilities, our sinful natures, or our mortality. We want men to be forever strong, powerful protectors. We want women to stay healthy, young, energetic, and attractive—not to mention selfless and nurturing.

What men and women need in one another, therefore, is an acceptance of our less-than-perfect selves and a willingness to accept our weaknesses and vulnerabilities. As long as we "never let them see us sweat," or "never let them see us cry," we won't achieve intimacy and openness in relationships.

All too often, men and women delve inside themselves and come up empty. We suffer from what we've come to term low self-image or poor self-esteem. More likely, I think, what we actually suffer from is a lack of knowledge about who we really are.

A couple of chapters ago I talked about the lost self—the inner person created in the image of God who sometimes is all but obliterated by shoulds and should nots, by rules, and by shame. If we are ever going to come to terms with who we are and develop healthy relationships, we must recover this lost self and be reconciled to the persons God created us to be. Which brings us back to Reconciliation Bay . . .

Too Many Dead Ends

The sun is just peeking over the mountain and streaming into our rooms, and another golden day beckons. Samantha is working with the counselor all morning, so we'll catch up with her a little later. I'm not sure where Kansas is this morning. I'm sure he'll turn up somewhere. But for now, it looks like it's just you and me.

The day is ours to wander about as we please. I'm heading down to the beach because that's where I get my most inspirational thoughts, and this chapter requires a great deal of inspiration as well as perspiration. I'd be pleased if you would join me.

As we begin our walk, the path twists and turns and branches out in a hundred directions. Some of the paths we try lead to the edge of the cliff; others wind down to a promontory point and stop at the edge of steep drop-offs. I'm beginning to wonder if any of these paths will take us where we want to go . . .

Getting down to that inviting beach, like getting into ourselves, can be a tricky business. It's easy to get lost trying to sort out who we are and what we're about. There's also a danger of becoming so involved in the search that we forget what we're looking for in the first place.

The Path to Healthy Self-Love

In all this focus on self-image and the lost self, you may be concerned that we are stepping into the forbidden zone of self-love often referred to as narcissism (after the Greek myth about Narcissus, who fell in love with his own reflection). And that concern is understandable. In fact, because it is difficult to distinguish between the God-created self and the human-created self, many Christian leaders are suspicious of the whole concept of healthy self-love.

Some Christians feel that to dig about one's inner self is akin to idol worship and that we should be practicing self-denial instead. One Christian counselor, Jay Adams, goes so far as to say that we are not supposed to be satisfied with ourselves as we are "but to destroy any satisfaction that may exist." He says, "You must treat yourself like a criminal, and put self to death every day."[3]

As a young Christian, I was taught that I should put the needs of others above my own and sacrifice my comforts for those less fortunate than I. I still believe that. At the same time, I was taught that people who love themselves are selfish. I *don't* believe that!

After all, the Bible says, ". . . no one ever hated his own body" (Ephesians 5:29 NIV). And Jesus said, ". . . love your neighbor as yourself" (Matthew 19:19 NIV). He didn't say "more than" or "instead of" but "as much as." If we hate our true selves, we hate the image God created.

Loving the Wrong Self

I would suggest that narcissism is not true self-love but rather a denial of the person we really are. One of our greatest gifts is the ability to know, respect, and love ourselves. Yet according to Alexander Lowen, "Narcissists do not love themselves or anyone else." Narcissism, Lowen says, "denotes a personality disturbance characterized by an exaggerated investment in one's self-image at the expense of the self."[4]

As I quote Dr. Lowen's concept of a narcissistic individual and a narcissistic culture, think about your own attitudes, those of people you know, and the attitudes of our culture today:

> Narcissists are more concerned with how they appear than what they feel . . . they deny feelings that contradict the image they seek. Acting without feeling, they tend to be seductive and manipulative, striving for power and control. They are egotists, focused on their own interests but lacking the true values of the self—namely self-expression, self-possession, dignity, and integrity. Narcissists lack a sense of self derived from body feelings. Without a solid sense of self, they experience life as empty and meaningless. It is a desolate state.[5]

Narcissism is the love and nurturance of a self created in the image we want the world to see, not love of the beautiful self created in God's image. Too much of what we read on self-esteem leads us falsely down this dead-end path of loving the wrong self.

A Lost Culture

It's especially difficult to sort out the truth when our whole society seems to be caught up in the worship of its false self! Lowen writes incisively of this culture in love with its wrong self:

> Narcissism can be seen in a loss of human values—in lack of concern for the environment, for the quality of life, for one's fellow human beings. A society that sacrifices the natural environment for profit and power betrays its sensitivity to human needs. The proliferation of material things becomes the measure of progress in living, and man is pitted against woman, worker against employer, individual against community. When wealth occupies a higher position than wisdom, when notoriety is admired more than dignity, when success is more important than self-respect, the culture itself overvalues "image" and must be regarded as narcissistic.[6]

Divorce, abortion, child abuse, pornography, murder, rape, the New Age quest for spiritual power—all are signs of this disintegration of values and preoccupation with a false image. Ours is a society that believes in its own false self, praising and glorifying what we fantasize we can become—not what we were meant to be. This love of a false image smacks of a desire to be godlike without being like God.

Created in the Image of God

If we become lost to the image of what God created us to be, Satan wins, just as he did in the Garden of Eden. As I mentioned earlier, when God created man and woman in His image, the humans could see that perfect image reflected in each other's and in God's eyes as they walked and talked with God in open camaraderie. God looked at them and said, "It is good."

Sadly, mankind didn't stay "good." Satan tempted Eve with knowledge that she could be better. By eating the forbidden fruit, he promised, she and her husband could attain equality with God. That's a lie, of course, but Eve believed it—as did Adam. And so instead of rejoicing in who they were as a son and daughter of the Creator, the first man and woman went beyond their human limits. We still do. And the result is that we experience the same feelings that plagued Adam and Eve—fear and shame. (See Genesis 2:25—3:11.)

John Bradshaw puts it this way: "The unconditional love and acceptance of self seems to be the hardest task for all humankind. Refusing to accept our 'real selves,' we try to create more powerful false selves or give up and become less than human. This results in a lifetime of cover-up and secrecy."[7]

A Journey Inward

That's why I feel the inward journey is important. Before we can be reconciled to God, we must dispose of the troublesome image we think we should be like and locate that person inside that God meant for us to be.

My strong feelings come out of personal experience. Before I could be reconciled to my husband and to the people around me in a meaningful way, I first had to be reconciled with myself.

I struggled for years to find ways to feel good about myself as a person. Due to my bout with unrealistic expectations in the Supermom era, I suffered from what everyone else seemed to have—a low self-esteem. I tried all the usual remedies:

- Forget about yourself—think of others. (This is wonderful advice so long as you are motivated by a sense of service rather than a desire to cover up things you don't like about yourself so others can see how good you are.)
- Forget others—think of yourself, because if you don't look out for yourself, who will? (Self-centered, navel-gazing, egomaniacs end up hating even themselves.)

- Cover the gray, make yourself over, get your colors done—a change in the outer package will give you a whole new outlook. (Why not? But don't expect the wrappings to change the inner you.)
- Affirm yourself every day—say catchy phrases like: "I am beautiful." "I'm a good person." "Inside me is a slim, trim gorgeous woman." (I tried affirmations, but all too often I felt I was just trying to brainwash myself.)

Each remedy helped for a time, but it all seemed so superficial. I could tell myself all kinds of wonderful things about me, and maybe some were true. But deep inside another voice kept saying, *You're not really beautiful. You're not basically a good person. You can cover the gray, wear great clothes, and change the way you look, but inside you're the same, unattractive, unacceptable person. You forgot yourself and thought of others and sacrificed yourself into a nervous breakdown—you're weak. And when you looked inside yourself you found nothing—because you* are *nothing.*

I knew the key to a healthy self-esteem was to love myself with an ease that allowed me then to forget me and concentrate on caring for others. But I couldn't seem to get to the place where I could accept myself, which made it extremely difficult to accept others.

Somehow I had to get to the truth. Was there anything to like about me? Could I ever have a healthy self-image? Could I ever find the path to the real me and stop pretending?

How about you? How do you feel about yourself? Are you searching for high self-esteem and finding that all the paths lead to dead ends? Personality Inventory 6 is a short quiz to help you determine your present direction.

Personality Inventory 6
Your Self-Esteem Checklist

	True	False
1. I experience a lot of dissatisfaction with myself.	☐	☐
2. I'm not very happy with my job or my job performance. (If you're a homemaker—that's your job!)	☐	☐
3. I feel as if I'm off target with my life.	☐	☐
4. I have a hard time loving myself.	☐	☐
5. I often feel as if I'm losing control.	☐	☐
6. I often feel isolated and stranded in my situation.	☐	☐
7. I try so hard and can't seem to get ahead. I feel like a failure.	☐	☐
8. Sometimes I think my family would be better off without me.	☐	☐
9. I need a change, but I'm afraid to try new things.	☐	☐
10. I often feel inadequate and would rather run away from problems than face them.	☐	☐
11. Sometimes I feel trapped by circumstances.	☐	☐
12. When I see how others are coping, I just get more depressed and discouraged with myself.	☐	☐
13. I feel as if I spend half my time pretending to be happy when I'm not.	☐	☐
14. I feel like an imposter.	☐	☐

If you marked most of the questions "true," chances are you are wandering along a maze of dead-end roads. If you ended up with more "false" answers, you're probably meandering a little closer to the path that leads to a healthier, happier self-esteem.

Finding the Right Trail

At one time in my life I was headed full speed on one of those dead-end roads. I knew I was lost, and I desperately needed a guide to point me in the right direction. It was like our trying to find the right path down to the beach here at Reconciliation Bay amid all these twists and turns . . .

"Where are you headed?" Kansas' familiar voice breaks my train of thought.

"Trying to discover which of these trails leads to the beach. I keep getting lost."

"It might help if you take your eyes off the path and look at the signs."

I sniff indignantly and stifle the urge to tell him what I think of his insolent remark. Then, as I raise my head, I see the weathered wooden arrow with the words *Beach Trail* carefully lettered on it.

Once again I have to admit Kansas is right. I've been keeping my nose to the ground, hurrying to get somewhere, and ending up nowhere.

As for finding my real self, I was too busy looking for answers inside myself when I should have been looking up, focusing on and seeking direction from God.

I had taken a lot of wrong turns before I finally took my eyes off the trail and looked upward. Then I saw the big picture. And I also discovered there was only one trail that would lead me to the real me. Digging around inside ourselves for answers as to who and what we are is fruitless. The answers will evade us unless we look upward and see self-esteem from God's perspective.

Seeing Yourself Through God's Eyes

A healthy self-esteem includes seeing ourselves as God sees us. (Remember, we can have no secrets from God. He knows every thought, every act, and every detail of our body, mind, and soul!)

The Bible gives us a clear picture of how God views us. Here are just a few examples:

Genesis 1:26–29

- We are created in God's image.
- We were created with intellect and the ability to communicate and to rule over the earth.
- God gives us power to make our own choices in life.
- "And God saw all that He had made; and behold, it was very good . . ." (v. 31).

Psalms 8:4–5

- He thinks about us and takes care of us.
- He designed us to be "a little lower than God."
- He crowns us with glory and majesty and has put all things under our feet.

John 3:16

- He loves us so much He sent His Son to die for our sins so that we could be reunited with Him.

John 14:1–3, 16

- He offers us eternal life with Him in heaven.
- He sends the Holy Spirit to guide and comfort us.

Hebrews 1:14

• God sends angels to watch over us.

The most important thing to realize is that we are so valuable to God that no sacrifice was too great to bring us back to the purity we had before sin destroyed our relationship with Him.

Knowing how God feels about me helped me realize that if I hate myself, I am, in a sense, calling God a liar. I didn't want to do that, but there were times I couldn't help feeling disappointed with the things I did and thought. With the innocence and open heart of a child, I asked God to help me understand. Then He gently took my hand and led me down the path of self-understanding and true self-love.

Finding the Real Me

The rocky footpath we've been traversing finally gives way to a white-gold, crescent-shaped beach. I drop my beach bag, shed my shoes, and give my feet a luxurious massage in the sun-warmed, sugar-fine sand. I glance at the shoreline and discover that the tide has left us a bounteous harvest of shells. With childlike enthusiasm I scurry off to collect every variety, size, shape, and color I can find—clams, scallops, conchs, abalones, moon snails, cowries, and whelks.

I lay out my treasures in the sand and pause to admire them. "Shells are like people," I remark.

"How's that?" Kansas replies.

"They're each unique and different. Look at all these scallops. At first, you might think they're all alike, but there are hundreds of different color variations and designs."

"Shells are like people in other ways, too," Kansas says, holding a large pink conch in his hand. "We live most of our lives hiding behind our protective shells."

"Sad, but true," I agree. "The shell is what everyone sees as the real you—or me—but it's only a thick, crusty coat of protection worn over the fragile, tender person inside."

"Even sadder is that if we're ever going to become a whole person with a healthy self-esteem, the shell has to go."

I shuddered. "It's a hard world out there, Kansas. I don't know if we can exist without some sort of protective cover."

"Maybe some people can't. But somehow I don't think we can afford to hold on to even a fragment of our false selves. Not if we want to be healthy and whole. Besides, it's not as if we're going out without any protection at all—we still have our natural, healthy defenses, and we have God. Being wrapped in His strength is a whole lot more secure than hiding behind any false image we can come up with."

Maybe Kansas is right. To really know who we are, we must step out of the shells of our false selves and walk into the world naked—willing to be real, vulnerable, and open.

When I slipped out of my shell a number of years ago, I was shocked at what I saw. The shell had not only protected me from others; it had served to hide me from myself. With the shell firmly in place, I had been able to ignore some of my undesirable qualities as well as my sinful nature.

Without the shell, I saw a part of me that was ugly and malformed. I wanted to put the shell back on so I wouldn't have to look. Then I remembered that it was in seeing me like this, tainted by sin, that Christ died for me.

We can love ourselves—our real selves—because Christ first loved us. We have healthy self-love when we:

· Accept ourselves as God's children—see that we are cherished, loved, and greatly valued by our Heavenly Father, in whose strength we can do all things.
· Give up our self-centeredness and stop lifting up, serving, protecting, and worshiping the false selves (shells) we create for our self-preservation.

• See ourselves as human beings created in God's image yet stained by sin and desperately in need of God's love, His redeeming grace and forgiveness.

It takes a strong sense of security and trust to shed the shells we've carried around for most of our lives. I've learned that shedding the false-self shell is possible when God surrounds us with the rock of His reality. But trusting in His strength is difficult for many of us. We may need a trip back into our childhood to learn how to do it.

Naked and Unashamed

You may think I'm minus a few brain cells, but when I get to the beach I have this enormous urge to take all my clothes off and run totally naked and uninhibited in the surf. The beach is a beautiful place for free spirits. However, since we are not entirely alone, I suggest we limit the stripping to shoes and socks.

The nakedness that really matters anyway is in our hearts, and God will see that, no matter what we wear.

So let your hair down and free yourself up a bit. Let's take a wild run on the beach. Let the wind run its fingers through your hair and take your breath away. For the moment, let's be like children again—free, unrestricted, all barriers shoved aside.

You may be asking, "Why all this childish free-spirit stuff?" And that's a valid question. I know this may seem silly to some of you. After all, it's hard to think in childhood terms when you've been persistently told to act your age. But who says that the ability to be free, uninhibited, and real must diminish with age?

The Lord specifically said that we must come to Him as children (see Mark 10:15), and I believe that as we break down our phony adult fortresses and allow the child in us to run free, we will indeed be able to see, accept, and love our real inner selves.

But can we:

> Become like a child again?
> Capture cloud creatures,
> touch the breeze,
> and bend rainbows?
> Play hide-and-seek in giant oaks
> and splash in rainy day puddles?
> Absurd!
> Or is it?
> Perhaps we could regain
> innocence . . .
> faith . . .
> trust.
> Trust ourselves . . .
> Our world . . .
> To God's grown-up hands.[8]

We can and we must, because the key to knowing and accepting our real self, the person created in God's image, is to discover the open, honest, vulnerable, and gifted child within us. The one who has no inhibitions, no pretense, no preconceived ideas about what should or shouldn't be—about what's possible and what's not.

At the beach I can find my childlike self. I can run in the surf, jump waves, and let my imagination soar as high as a kite on the wind. On my own inward journey, it has been these fanciful beach trips, where I have loosened up my restraints and become a child again, that have led me to a healthy self-esteem. It is here that I, in childlike awe and reverence, have been able to see myself through God's eyes.

When we follow the right trail, discard our exterior shells, become more childlike, and become reconciled to our God-created selves by seeing ourselves through God's eyes, we are well on the way toward healthy self-love and self-acceptance.

Clean and Whole

I'm very content at the moment, lying here on the white-gold sand of Reconciliation Bay. The tide is coming in, and I let the water wash over me. I see the cleansing water wash away the footprints and the debris, leaving the shore pure and unblemished. I sense, as I pause to give myself up to the Father, that I, too, am washed, cleansed, and renewed.

When you come to know, understand, accept, and love yourself in a healthy way, you can walk into your relationship as a whole individual, separate and distinctly different from your partner.

Whole persons have a healthy love for their families and have moved from dependence to independence—or to what psychologists call "individuation." They have become different from, yet still associated with, those they love. John Bradshaw tells us:

> Being individuated does not mean that each does not need the other to love and care for. It means that while desiring to love and care for each other and to be loved and cared for by each other, each knows they can survive alone. Each knows he is responsible for his own life and happiness. Each knows that the other can't make him happy. Each knows that the other is *not* his better half. Differentiation means that each partner has worked through his own fantasy bond.[9]

I think that's one of the things the apostle Paul had in mind when he wrote that Christians should "not be conformed to this world" (Romans 12:2). Instead of being trapped by the rigid rules of a culture or the unhealthy boundaries of a dysfunctional family, we are called to "be transformed" (differentiated) into God's image. With that differentiation, we have the freedom to move forward into any relationship without fear of rejection or failure.

Up From the Beach

It's beautiful on the beach, but we cannot lie here forever. Once we have reconciled to ourselves, we move on to confront another area I see as vital to our growth as individuals and as couples: reconciliation to others. For as important as gaining a healthy appreciation for self is, it is only a starting point. M. Scott Peck points out in his book *The Different Drum*, we "can never be completely whole in and of ourselves. We cannot be all things to ourselves and others . . . we are inevitably social creatures who desperately need each other not merely for sustenance, not merely for company, but for any meaning in our lives whatsoever."[10]

As we make our way back from the beach, Samantha greets us with a warm smile and an enthusiasm I haven't seen in her before. She falls into step with Kansas.

"I take it you've had a good day," he says, draping an arm comfortably across her shoulders.

"It was wonderful. I learned some important facts about alcoholism and addictive behavior that helped me understand why my parents behaved the way they did and why I have such a hard time trusting men."

"Then you've forgiven them?"

"It isn't that easy. Let's just say I'm working on it."

"What about David?"

"The counselor worked with me on some of my dysfunctional beliefs."

"Such as?"

"My need to be in control, thinking that no one could like me, having unrealistic expectations of myself and others. Things like that. I made a lot of mistakes with David." Sam chewed on her lower lip. "I was wrong to depend on the computer to choose someone for me; I should have listened to my heart and to God. I just hope it isn't too late."

Chapter 13
Reconciling With
One Another

DAVID STIRRED, sensing another presence in the room. He opened his eyes slowly. A woman stood before him dressed in white. A riot of red curls framed a serene face. "An angel," he mumbled through a mouth that felt dry and cottony. "I've died and gone to heaven."

The vision laughed. "I certainly hope not. I'd have a hard time trying to explain why I'm talking to a corpse." She placed a tray of vials and syringes on the bedside tray table. "Actually, a vampire would be more like it." She gave him a wicked smile, dropped her voice, and with a Transylvanian accent said, "I've come to take your blood."

David groaned. As she applied the tourniquet to his arm, he read her name tag: *Ms. Smith, RN, Nurse Specialist.* "I don't remember seeing you around here before. Are you new? What's a nurse specialist?"

"I don't work for the hospital, and no, you haven't seen me before. I'm a free-lancer. I specialize in caring for people like you who insist on going home before the doctor is ready to discharge them."

"I'm afraid I don't understand."

"It's simple, really. You've insisted on leaving today, to fly off to some island that doesn't even have a phone. I've been hired to stick to you like glue until I'm sure you get the rest and the care you need. I cater to spoiled businessmen like yourself who don't know the meaning of rest and relaxation. And don't try to duck out on me—I can run a lot faster than a man on crutches, and I'm considerably stronger than I look."

She looked . . . nice, David decided, and he shrugged off his feelings of annoyance at having his life interfered with. He found himself thinking he might enjoy this traveling companion who'd been assigned, by his mother no doubt, to care for him. He winced as Ms. Smith expertly slid the large-gauge needle into his vein and withdrew two vials of blood. "Anything else you'd like to sample while you're at it?" he teased, letting himself indulge in a little flirtation.

"Look, Mr. Hartley"—her smile faded—"I have a good sense of humor, and I certainly enjoy a little innocent bantering, but let's get something straight. You're a married man, and I understand the reason for this trip is so you can get back to your wife and finish up your honeymoon. I'll assume your innuendo is a result of your sexual frustration, and if you promise to be on your best behavior toward me, I promise not to tell your wife what a flirt you are."

David stared at her a moment, feeling resolutely put in his place and a little stunned at her overreaction. "I'm sorry . . . I didn't mean . . . but you're right; that was uncalled for."

A sheepish grin tugged at the corners of her mouth. "I guess I should apologize too—for coming on so strong. I meant what I said, though. I . . . I just don't have much tolerance for men who don't take their marriage vows seriously."

She had been hurt. David read it in her eyes. Maybe sometime during their long trip he'd ask her about it. "I take my marriage seriously," he said. "I just wish I could be sure my wife felt the same way."

She met his eyes and his torment seemed to match her own. Perhaps she had judged him too harshly. He was a nice man, but Jill had no interest in men. Except for one. But thank God there was too much to do now to think about *him*.

Several hours later, David and his nurse strapped themselves into their first-class seats. According to their schedule, they'd fly into San Diego and transfer to a helicopter for the rest of the flight. David had dozed off, exhausted from the flurry of activity. Jill touched his flushed cheek, thankful that the doctor had written a prescription for antibiotics as well as pain medication.

After making certain her patient was comfortable, Jill leaned her head back into the seat. She let her mind dwell on the man who had once been her husband . . . tall, wavy brown hair, and twinkling brown eyes that seemed as vivid in her imagination as they had five years ago. Then she remembered the shock in those eyes, the mixture of horror, fear, and disgust when he had hit her. Kansas hadn't meant to hurt her; she knew that. If only he'd stayed, she would have told him it was okay, that she understood, and that with counseling they would work it out together. But he hadn't stayed. He'd walked out and never returned.

David touched her arm to draw her back from the unhappy place where she had apparently withdrawn.

"Wha—oh, I'm sorry. I was just thinking about Kansas . . . ah . . . never mind. Did you need something?"

"Kansas?" David tightened his hold on her arm.

Jill stared at him and twisted her arm out of his grasp. "I . . ."

"Smith . . . of course! You're Jill, aren't you? You're his wife."

She frowned, suddenly feeling as though she had been thrust into some kind of twilight zone.

"I can't believe this," David went on. "You set this up, didn't you?"

"I don't . . ." Jill shook her head and took a moment to gather her wits about her. "Wait a minute." She took a deep breath and let it out slowly. She was a professional, but even thinking about Kansas Smith was enough to turn her world into chaos. "Please tell me what you're talking about. How do you know about Kansas and me? And what am I supposed to have set up?"

"Kansas is a close friend of mine. He told me about you—about what happened. Are you trying to tell me you don't know where he is?"

"No, I don't. I haven't seen or heard from him since he left five years ago."

"Jill, we're heading for Reconciliation Bay. I'm going there to meet my wife and your husband, Kansas Smith."

Oh, What a Tangled Web . . .

The web that's been woven around the lives of Samantha and David, Kansas and Jill is a tangled one—but not, as the old saying goes, a web meant to deceive. Rather, it is a net filled with emotions—pride, insecurities, pain, bittersweet love—the kinds of threads life weaves in, among, and around us every day.

I know what you're thinking: The old happy-ever-after ending is coming any minute now. The chopper will land, and David will run into Samantha's arms, smother her with kisses, and carry her over a threshold of eternal bliss. Jill and Kansas will gaze into each other's eyes and, with arms entwined, walk lazily into paradise.

I do like happy endings, but if you were thinking I'd use this chapter to pour out a syrupy, fairy tale reunion, you're wrong. Actually, what I have in mind is . . . well, why don't we return to the story and find out.

On board the helicopter, Jill closed her eyes as the shock waves rolled over her. This couldn't be happening to her. She and Kimberly lived an orderly, sane life. She was a nurse and a devoted mother to the child Kansas had left behind. Born eight months after Kansas left, Kimberly was a delight and a constant reminder of her father. How would Kansas feel about a child? Would she even tell him?

Fear, anger, joy, love, hate all tumbled around in her mind. Five years she had waited for the day she would see Kansas again. She had played the scene over and over in her mind, rehearsing what she would say. Sometimes she envisioned herself running into his arms. Other times she saw herself slapping his arrogantly handsome face and thrusting divorce papers into his hands. She should have divorced him long ago, but she had never been able to take that final step.

"We're landing," David said, touching her shoulder.

"Oh." She managed no more than a whisper. With her heart thudding against her chest like a jackhammer, Jill glanced down at the group of people who had come out to the landing pad. Kansas stood among them, taller than the rest. She wasn't sure what she had expected, and she felt a growing resentment that his presence could still affect her so strongly.

She forced her gaze away from Kansas and onto the woman who stood next to him. David's wife. She recognized her from a photo David had shown her. As she watched, Kansas wrapped a possessive arm around Samantha's shoulder as if he were staking a claim to his territory.

Well, after five years it was only natural that Kansas should find another woman. But why this one? Jill looked away, hoping her patient hadn't seen the intimate gesture. The hard set of his jaw told her he had.

"It looks like we're too late." David's words were strained, clearly edged with anger and a pain no medication would relieve.

She would have to put Kansas out of her mind now; it was something she knew how to do quite well. David was her patient, but she hadn't anticipated the kind of complications this meeting might entail.

"Stay here," Jill commanded. "I'll get someone to help you out." David didn't need the order. The eagerness to see Samantha vanished in the flames of his quiet fury.

Before the blades had stopped swirling, Jill climbed out of the helicopter. In an instant Kansas was beside her. It took all the control she could muster to look at him.

"Jill?" He blinked and stared at her. He wanted to touch her, wrap her in his arms, and welcome her, but he couldn't—not yet. He had to know if she still cared about him.

"Kansas," she said, surprised at the composed flatness in her voice, "David told me on the flight that you were here. He's been hurt, and I need a couple of men to lift him out and into his wheelchair."

Kansas frowned, puzzled—no, disappointed—by her coldness. Finally her words sliced their way into his confused mind. "David? Hurt? What happened?"

"I'm sure he'll explain everything later."

Jill moved away, but Kansas didn't follow. He'd have to deal with her later. With the pilot's help, Kansas lowered David to the ground and into the wheelchair, then pushed him clear of the landing pad and over to where Samantha stood. The air crackled with tension.

Samantha couldn't speak. She wanted to fling herself into his arms and tell him how she had come to love him, how everything was changing for her, how she was being healed. But the hardness in his eyes silenced her, and Sam wondered if the only reason David had come back was to say good-bye. She felt a hand on her arm and stiffened.

"Mrs. Hartley, I'm Jill Smith, David's nurse. If you could show me where David will be staying, we'll get him settled."

"I'll take care of it," Kansas offered gruffly before Sam could answer. He maneuvered the chair onto the path leading to the Sanctuary. They walked together, yet separate. Four minds filled with confusing thoughts . . . four hearts aching to be reconciled . . . and four mouths silenced by pride and fear of what each of the others might have to say.

*   *   *

Conversations are stilted through dinner. Every time I look up, Kansas glares at me as if he holds me responsible for this strange turn of events. He catches up with me that evening as I settle myself into a lounge chair in the garden to watch the stars come out.

"Why did you bring her here?" Kansas asks as he pulls a chair close to mine. He lowers himself into it and leans forward, holding his head in his hands.

"I thought it would make you happy."

"Happy? You thought it would make me happy to see Jill involved with David? I'm overjoyed, can't you tell? Just when I thought David and Samantha were finally going to make it. Samantha was just beginning to trust again—you destroyed her."

"Sam is stronger than you think. And what makes you think Jill and David are an item? Did she tell you?"

"I'd be a fool not to notice that she hasn't let him out of her sight. She's fluttering around him like a mother hen."

"She's his nurse," I answer.

"If there's nothing going on between David and Jill, why are we all so miserable?"

I smile, feeling a little smug that after all these chapters the tables have turned and I can offer him advice. "Kansas," I say, "lean back in your chair and close your eyes."

He glares at me, and for a minute I'm afraid he's going to refuse. Then, after a deep, shaky sigh, he does as he's been told.

"Why are you here?"

"I came out to give you a piece of my mind."

"An exercise in futility since, as you are one of my characters, I already know your mind—most of it anyway."

"Don't remind me." He pauses.

"I mean, why are you here in this book?"

"As a guide. My job is to show people the sights, to point out areas of interest and offer sage advice when the opportunity arises. I act as a sort of liaison between the real and unreal."

"And now?"

"I'm frustrated, confused. I'm angry with you. I'm angry with myself . . . I wish . . ."

"What do you wish?"

"That I had just scooped Jill up in my arms when she got off that chopper and run off into the woods with her."

"You Tarzan?"

"Yeah." A smile tugs at the corners of his mouth.

"Then what?"

"I'd set her down in the top of a tree and make her listen to me. I'd apologize for being such a jerk. I'd ask her to tell me about her life." His voice softened and slowed. "And ask her if we couldn't give it another try."

"Do you love her?"

"Aha! What an idiot I am." Kansas straightens and hits the palm of his hand against his forehead. "This is a test. Right? You want to know if I practice what I preach. And I blew it. One look at Jill, and I fell to pieces. I jumped to conclusions and imagined all sorts of scenarios. This chapter is on reconciling with one another. She's here, and that can only mean one thing. You want this book to have a happy ending. All I have to do is talk to her, and everything will work out. And if I can remember to say and do all the right things, we'll be together forever. That's it, isn't it?"

I wince. "Not exactly. Yes, I think it would be wise if you talked. All four of you have broken the number-one rule in communication: you've based your conclusions on assumptions rather than facts. And it's true that Reconciliation Bay is a place for resolutions. But I can't promise a happy ending—that's up to you and Jill."

Suddenly I wish Jill hadn't been assigned to care for David, that she had stayed back in the States. I wonder how this chapter will get written if Kansas doesn't stabilize and settle back into his important role as our spiritual guide and interpreter.

"Kansas," I say after a long silence.

"What?"

I point to a lone figure who has emerged from a grove of trees on the other end of the garden. We watch as she lowers herself into a lawn swing and leans her head against the oak slats. Kansas rises slowly and walks across the long expanse of lawn to join her.

I lean back into the lounge chair again and look up into the sky, wondering what the outcome will be. Frankly, I'm a little disappointed that Kansas turned out to be as unpredictable and vulnerable as the rest of us. I might have known. Obviously, it would have taken a perfect mind to create a perfect character or plot. Well, since Kansas is busy reconciling his own relationship, I guess the burden of responsibility for presenting ways of resolving irreconcilable differences comes back to me.

Together, Yet Separate

As I gaze into the heavens, a million stars hang suspended in a dark velvet sky, clustering in constellations. The Big Dipper, the Southern Cross, Orion—all are woven into the fabric of the universe by an almighty and omnipotent God. Together, the stars in each constellation create a unit—a picture pleasing to the senses. Each is equal in importance, separate, alone. They are light-years apart. And yet they are together.

Men and women, too, are equal and separate entities, created to merge into one fabric known as humanity. Like individual stars in a constellation, they were united for a purpose. Together they share the universe, and each has a unique role according to his or her abilities and talents.

Sadly, the fabric of human unity has been torn asunder by irreconcilable differences between God and Satan, men and women; between mothers and daughters, fathers and sons; between clans and nations. Unable to resolve and accept our differences, we become separated and isolated.

In our exploration of Reconciliation Bay, we've discovered

that what men and women need most in each other is to develop an intimate relationship with God. Without unity with the Creator, we will always feel a deep, aching hunger, a perpetual dissatisfaction, and be constantly looking over the fence for something better than what we have.

A second basic need we've explored is the need to put away the selves we have created in our own minds and to find and come to love our real childlike, vulnerable selves created in God's image. For until we can love, understand, and accept ourselves for who we are, we can't fully love and accept others.

In this chapter we come to a third basic need—the need to be reconciled to others. Such reconciliation means much more than just "getting back together" in a single man-woman relationship—although that's part of it. Reconciling to others more basically means coming together as a people united by God to fulfill His purpose on earth.

Before we can attempt to live with one person for a lifetime, I feel it is essential that we learn where and how we fit in the constellation called humankind. We must first acknowledge our importance as a part in the constellation, then learn how to enjoy, appreciate, accept, respect, and love our neighbors—all the other "stars" that hang together to make a whole. Just as we cannot be all things to ourselves, neither can we expect one person—even a spouse—to meet all our needs.

Being Part of a Whole

I am a single star, as are you. God has chosen to link us together in a constellation known as humankind. But what is my part? Where do I fit? What is my purpose?

In the last chapter we talked about self-acceptance and about the importance of discovering the true self created in God's image. But the purpose of discovering who we really are is so that we might fulfill God's plan for us. Our fulfillment or wholeness will come as we offer all that we have to whatever position God has placed us in.

A star fills a particular space, and it twinkles. In the constellation of which I am a part, my role, too, is to twinkle—to give what God has given me for the betterment of the community of which I am an intricate part. And that community is not a city or a building but rather the network of people God places in my space on any given day.

Oswald Chambers, in his classic book *My Utmost for His Highest*, tells us:

> We are not out for our own cause at all, we are out for the cause of God, which can never be our cause. We do not know what God is after, but we have to maintain our relationship with Him whatever happens—we must never allow anything to injure our relationship with Him. . . . The main thing about Christianity is not the work we do, but the relationships we maintain and the atmosphere produced by that relationship.[1]

Each person's God-given role in the human community is different. I think of Mother Teresa of Calcutta, for instance, and see God's love fulfilled. For many years, this beautiful woman of God has given her life in sacrificial love for others. Her life is Christ's, and her body is a true temple of the Lord.

My life isn't as exemplary as Mother Teresa's. I don't live in the slums as she does or care for lepers. I live in the United States in a nice house where Ron and I reared two children. The only slums I minister in seem to be the devastated ruins in people's hearts. The only lepers I care for are those people I meet as a counselor—those who struggle with emotional diseases which make them feel unclean, unwanted, isolated, and worthless.

Yet this is my space, the place God has given me for now to fulfill my role in the constellation of humanity. And as I try to live for Him in my place, Christ lives in me, too.

God's message for our purpose is clear as we come to understand Jesus Christ and strive to be like Him. We find instructions in Scripture passages such as Luke 6:35–37:

> Love your enemies, and do good, and lend, expecting nothing in return; and your reward will be great, and you will be sons [and daughters] of the Most High; for He Himself is kind to ungrateful and evil men. Be merciful, just as your Father is merciful. And do not pass judgment and you will not be judged; and do not condemn, and you shall not be condemned; pardon, and you will be pardoned.

It is in this spirit of love and service that we come into reconciliation with others—not considering what we can receive but rather what we can give. We are called to serve as individual units who together create a constellation that is pleasing to the world and to God. We join together then as individuals, alike yet separate, each joyfully involved in our unique tasks, to form friendships or communities in which we share our lives with people who have a common goal.

The Necessary Element of Community

Perhaps you're wondering why the emphasis on community and on working together. It's because no matter how self-sufficient or adept we are, we need the companionship of others. Oh, not constantly, of course. But frequently, consistently, we do need each other. God understands our need for companionship. At the beginning of human life, He said, ". . . It is not good for the man to be alone. I will make a helper suitable for him" (Genesis 2:18 NIV).

As psychologist Scott Peck writes:

> Trapped in our tradition of rugged individualism, we are an extraordinary lonely people. . . . Look at the sad, frozen faces all

around you and search in vain for the souls hidden behind masks of make-up, masks of pretense, masks of composure. . . . We are desperately in need of a new ethic of "soft individualism," an understanding of individualism which teaches that we cannot be truly ourselves until we are able to share freely the things we most have in common: our weakness, our incompleteness, our imperfection, our inadequacy, our sins, our lack of wholeness and self sufficiency. . . . It is a kind of softness that allows those necessary barriers, or outlines, of our individual selves to be like permeable membranes, permitting ourselves to seep out and the selves of others to seep in.[2]

Community, then, is a melding together of our "soft individualism" to create a safe place in which we can grow together—a place which promotes openness and intimacy with one another.

But how can we maintain that kind of community? Anyone who has ever lived with anyone else knows it's not easy. We need one another; we need companionship. But sometimes our words and actions push others away. We have difficulty getting along with friends, marriage partners, and business associates, and all too often we end up alone, rejected, and incomplete.

In the next few pages I'd like to explore six key factors to preserving community and relationships: equality, communication, conflict resolution, commitment, intimacy, and love. These won't provide all the answers, of course, but they are a good place to start.

Equality Is a State of Being

Let's take the topic of equality first, because I see a great many relationships fall apart in the power struggle over equal rights and a striving for fulfillment. That is an unfortunate and completely unnecessary struggle, because no relationship—not even marriage—should be allowed to eliminate one's individuality or identity.

My equality is not measured by how much I am paid or how ruthlessly I have fought my way up a corporate ladder. Equality isn't something you achieve; it is something you are. Yet even today, with all the work that has been done to assure our equal rights, there are men *and* women who see women as less important—less equal—than men.

This is simply not valid! As Phyllis Schlafly states in her book *The Power of the Christian Woman*, "Being sexually and physically different from man, and complementary to man does not in any sense make woman less of a human being in God's image. It does not make her inferior in God's love or inferior to man. Like man, woman was given an immortal soul, an intellect, and a free will."[3] God will hold both men and women responsible for their actions.

In the Bible, both the apostle Paul and Jesus Christ are strong advocates of women. In fact, Paul specifically encouraged women in their ministries. Romans 16:1–2, for instance, reads, "I commend to you our sister Phoebe, a deaconess of the church at Cenchreae, that you may receive her in the Lord as befits the saints, and help her in whatever she may require from you, for she has been a helper of many and of myself as well" (RSV). I could cite many other examples but instead will recommend a wonderful book that I believe will help clarify the biblical roles of women and men, *The Apostle Paul and Women in the Church*, by Don Williams.[4]

Before we can work together in unity, we must acknowledge that men and women are of equal importance to God. Being equal in importance, however, does not necessarily mean an even division of roles and responsibilities. One experienced couple, married since 1939, said in an interview, "Marriage isn't a give and take proposition. You don't give 50 percent and expect 50 percent in return. You give 100 percent for both sides. Don't be trying to divvy it up."[5]

Equality in relationships does, on the other hand, open the doors to freedom for each partner to be listened to and understood. Which leads us into a second aspect of maintaining relationships—communication.

Tell Me What You're Thinking

I avert my gaze from the stars and glance for a moment at the two figures occupying the lawn swing. I'm pleased at what I see. Even in the dim moonlight, I can see that Kansas is intently listening to what Jill is saying.

What Kansas and Jill and David and Samantha and men and women across America need most in each other is someone who will listen to them and accept and respect their opinions. In fact, I believe that effective communication is the single most important element in relationships. I could write a whole book on communication, but due to lack of time and space, I will just outline a few basic principles.

Let's start with examining some communication blockers. The list of chief offenders includes:

- Assumption ("I know what you're thinking.")
- Interruption (Failing to listen, and disallowing explanations of feelings and thoughts.)
- Attacking (Using unfair fight tactics such as threats, placing blame, labeling, name-calling, and bringing up unrelated past incidences.)

Here is an example of these communication blockers in action. Richard and Marge are planning a vacation. He has suggested that they leave the children with relatives and go alone. Marge responds with a contemplative, "Hmmm."

"I know what you're thinking," Richard says. "You think I'm selfish because I don't want to take the kids to Hawaii with us."

Scenario #1

There are several ways Marge might respond to this. Say, perhaps, that she gets defensive and retorts with something like,

"Oh, yeah? Well, who made you a mind reader? If you're so all-knowing, why don't you get a job with the CIA? Maybe they would appreciate your talent—I don't. You always think you know what I think, and you're always wrong. Do you want to know what I really think?"

Such a remark deserves even greater criticism than Richard's original one because it is defensive, childish, off the subject, insulting, and untrue. (Richard doesn't *always* tell her what she thinks.)

Scenario #2

Or Marge might respond this way: With tears in her eyes, she sinks back into the cushions. Hurt, anger, and resentment force their way into her heart, but she pushes them back. If that's what he thinks, then fine.

Richard's fire is fueled by her silence, and he presumes he's right in his assessment. "Well, if I'm so selfish, then maybe I should go to Hawaii alone. I'm sure there are other women who would think differently."

Marge builds an even thicker wall with silence than she does with harsh words. She affirms in her mind that her husband is a brute. "Go ahead and leave if that's what you want. Any woman stupid enough to put up with you can have you."

Naturally, Richard communicates his disgust as he stomps out of the house and slams the door behind him.

Scenario #3

Now suppose the conversation were to go this way:
"Hmmm."

"I know what you're thinking," Richard says. "You think I'm selfish because I don't want to take the kids to Hawaii with us."

"No. I apologize if my hesitation caused you to think that. Actually, I was thinking that our going to Hawaii was a romantic suggestion. My hesitation was due to concern over how we might find someone to watch four kids for two weeks."

"You don't think I was being selfish?"

"No," Marge laughs, "I think it's the most wonderful idea you've ever had. Now let's figure out what to do with the kids."

I don't know about you, but I definitely choose #3! Richard's careless assumption and Marge's response could have sent them to divorce court instead of on a second honeymoon in Hawaii. Careful communication can prevent a misunderstanding from escalating into a full-fledged battle.

Take Time to Listen

No one appreciates being told what he or she thinks. Whether the other person is right or wrong—and they are very often wrong!—it's unfair and rude to assume you know another person's thoughts. All too often our assumptions about another's thoughts come as a result of our own insecurities and fears rather than from facts. Our thoughts about others are often tainted by the way we picture ourselves, or by internal "parent tapes" or patterns left over in our minds from childhood. Good communication comes when we deliberately set aside our prejudices, our defense systems, and objectively listen to what others have to say.

I wonder how many conflicts within a relationship could be resolved if each person could say, "Tell me what you're thinking," then take time to listen and understand.

When two people live together, conflict is inevitable. We will do well, before we even begin to attempt better communication with someone, to tune our minds to certain facts of life:

· Not everyone will agree with my point of view.
· People differ according to their gender, their personalities, backgrounds, cultures, emotions, viewpoints, and approaches to life.

- It takes two people (or more) to fight.
- Conflict *can* be resolved.

Resolving Conflict

We've seen and experienced some major communication blockers and noted that conflict is a given in any relationship. Now let's review six guidelines for resolving conflict and enhancing communication:

1. *Admit your responsibility* in the conflict rather than placing blame. Ask yourself:

- What have I done or not done to cause this problem?
- Have I been critical or hurtful?
- What is my attitude, my facial expression?
- What tone of voice did I use?
- Am I passively running away from the conflict?
- Am I being pushy and aggressive?
- What can I do to resolve the problem?

2. *Be willing to change your views and your ways* if that change will be mutually advantageous to your relationship.

3. *Don't allow anger to control you*—although you can express it and dispel it in healthy ways. That means verbally (i.e., "I feel angry when you . . ."), not by throwing things!

4. *Refrain from opening past hurts and wounds.* Don't dump old or unrelated issues onto the problem at hand.

5. *Concentrate on the present and on possible solutions rather than on past failures.*

6. *Avoid dropping emotional bombs*—"loaded" words and accusations such as *always, never, stupid, dumb, childish, pigheaded,* and so on.

7. *Think about what you want to say and how it will affect your partner before you speak.*

8. *Ask, "What are you thinking?" "What are you feeling?"* Then

listen. Scott Peck says, "True listening, total concentration on the other, is always a manifestation of love. An essential part of true listening is the . . . temporary giving up or setting aside of one's own prejudices, frames of references and desires so as to experience as far as possible the speaker's world from the inside, stepping inside his or her shoes."[6]

9. *Don't collect resentments or pieces of unfinished business.* Forgive and forget, to the degree possible, the put-downs, rejections, misunderstandings, and disappointments others have piled on your head over the years. Dragging along the old baggage hinders your ability to communicate clearly and effectively. Jesus has offered to take your burdens on His shoulders. Let Him.

10. *Listen and speak in love.* "If I speak with the tongues of men and of angels, but do not have love, I have become a noisy gong or a clanging cymbal" (1 Corinthians 13:1). But when I communicate in a loving way, I am patient, kind, and not jealous. I do not brag and am not arrogant; neither do I act unbecomingly or seek my own way. If I listen and speak in love, I will not be provoked, nor will I take into account a wrong suffered. Rather than rejoice in my partner's unfairness, injustice, and inappropriateness, I will seek and rejoice in the truth—in finding solutions (vv. 4–6, author's paraphrase). Love ". . . bears all things, believes all things, hopes all things, endures all things. Love never fails" (vv. 7–8).

Learning effective methods of communication may cost us considerable time and effort, but if it helps us get along better with those we love, it will be well worth the price.

Commitment

Beyond good communication is the desire and drive to make relationships last. I look again at the stars hanging over Reconciliation Bay and note that the constellations have hung together for an eternity—committed to the time and space in which God placed them.

Commitment is a God-created bond that unites human beings to Himself, to one another, and to the earth so that life can be accomplished. It is a stubbornness that grows out of love. It is mysterious, sturdy, faithful, generous, honest, and long-suffering.

I think of the many torn places and frayed edges I see in the fabric of my own part of the universe—in my own marriage. The misunderstandings we've had, the changes we've tried to make in each other shredded the fragile threads of our existence. We're mending now. And I sense that some of the patched-over places make us stronger and more wearable than ever before. What is it that holds our relationship together?

Faithfulness formed a "Super Glue®" that has held Ron and I together for over twenty-five years. When I surveyed men and women for views on what men and women needed most in each other, commitment always hit the top ten.

Just as it takes more than one person to create an argument, it takes the decision of more than one person to create the bond of commitment. Both Ron and I chose to love each other—and we have repeated that decision over and over through the years. And it has not always been an easy choice. Sure, we had our honeymoon phase, but romantic love is filled with fickle emotions and perishable ingredients and is more like cake frosting than Super Glue®. (It's sweet and pretty, but eventually it crumbles.) Somewhere along the way we switched adhesives and chose to stick together, hopefully forever.

My thoughts scatter as footsteps sound along the garden path. "How's it going?" Kansas asks. Moonlight dances in his eyes, and I can tell his conversation with Jill was a fruitful one.

"Fine," I reply. "I just finished the segment on commitment—speaking of which . . . how did your talk go?"

"You mean you don't know?"

"Give me a break—I've only got one mind. I've been too busy getting into constellations, companions, and communication to think about your conversation with Jill."

Kansas chuckles, lowers himself into the lounge chair beside me, and crosses his long legs. To add to his cocky appearance, he flips his Akubra down to cover half his face. "Then I think I'll let you go on guessing," he says, his grin barely visible beneath the leather rim.

"Suit yourself." I shrug. "If you don't tell me, I'll just make something up."

My remark must have gotten to him, because he's sitting straight up and leaning in my direction before I can take my next breath. His hand shoots out to grab my arm. "No, don't do that. With my luck you'll have us fighting again."

It's my turn to laugh. "Okay, I'll leave your script alone and you can tell me about it later. I was just finishing this material on commitment. Is there anything you'd like to add?"

"Just one thing. When you commit yourself to a marriage, get married with the feeling it's going to last. Don't be like the bride who 'doubled the wedding cake recipe and froze one for the second time around.' "[7]

"Where did you get that?" I ask in mock disgust.

"From *Phyllis Diller's Marriage Manual*. You want to hear another one?"

"No!" I laugh and say, "I'm beginning to wonder if falling in love again has given you a concussion. I think I'll handle the rest of this chapter alone. Say good night, Kansas."

"Good night, Kansas," he says irreverently as he climbs out of the chair and saunters up the walk to the Sanctuary. The tune he whistles leaves no doubt in my mind. The man is completely and irrevocably smitten.

With the whistled rendition of "I'm Sitting On Top of the World" fading in the background, I settle myself in the chair again and turn my mind over to the task at hand. The next important facet of companionship is intimacy. And I can't help thinking that a good example of intimacy is the bantering that just went on between Kansas and me.

234

Intimacy

Intimacy is sharing one's deepest and personal parts with another. This intimacy may or may not be expressed sexually. In fact, the intimate moments dearest to my heart have nothing whatever to do with sexual intercourse. When I recall intimate moments in my own life I think of:

- . . . when I was five years old and Daddy and I (on one of his brief visits home from the hospital) wished on a turkey wishbone that he would get well and stay home. We broke it and I won.
- . . . when I placed our newborn son in the tender cradle of my wary husband's powerful arms.
- . . . when I felt depressed and lonely and my husband held me on his lap and rocked me.
- . . . when my grandchild lay down beside me in the grass and asked, "Nana, why is grass green?"
- . . . when my prayer group rejoiced over Dottie's healing.
- . . . when we cried over Jackie's death.
- . . . whenever I sit alone with God.

In true intimacy we share the depths of our being with others without fear of rejection. In intimacy we accept one another's secrets and treat them as priceless treasures. One of the greatest needs of men and women is the need to share this kind of intimacy.

Love

Men and women also need unfailing love. Not a wild tempestuous passion that sends our senses reeling and puts our minds out to lunch but a deliberate, stubborn, choosing kind of love. The love men and women need as they seek to maintain and establish relationships is absolute, complete, decisive, and final:

Love is blind, the phrase runs.
Nay, I would rather say,
love sees as God sees,
and with infinite wisdom
has infinite pardon.[8]

Love means looking at one another accurately, acknowledging faults and seeing beyond them. Love welcomes companionship, sees value in all people, listens, commits, and accepts.

Someone once said, "Love is the doorway through which the human soul passes from selfishness to service and from solitude to kinship with all mankind." And that epitomizes what both men and women need most: to be reconciled—to be at peace with God, with self, and with one another.

At the End of the Day

It's getting late. I've watched the stars far too long, and I really must go. There's packing to be done and good-byes to be said. Tomorrow morning the *Kristiana* will be hoisting anchor and sailing for home. I wish I could stay here in this restful place. But every day, every dream, every vacation, and every book must come to an end.

So it's time to gather up our bits and pieces of information and the remnants of our stories and head into the final, homeward leg of our journey.

Chapter 14
Going Home

THE SUNRISE ON Reconciliation Bay cast a rose-colored hue across the landscape. Samantha rose from her solitary bed and walked to the window.

"Oh, no!" she gasped. Stunned, she watched David hobbling toward the helicopter on crutches. She had expected him to go home on the *Kristiana*. She had hoped they would be able to talk and make another attempt at straightening out their lives. He was alone, and Samantha briefly wondered where Jill had gone. But his aloneness gave her the edge she needed.

Sam slipped on a bathrobe and ran out of the room, down the stairs, and out of the Sanctuary. The graveled path dug into her bare feet, slowing her progress. As she cleared the lawn's tree-lined edge and came within sight of the launching pad, she shouted to him, but he didn't hear—or didn't want to.

David hoisted himself into the aircraft. He was leaving Reconciliation Bay and all that it stood for, along with the painful reminder that Sam no longer wanted him. Once seated, he strapped himself in and signaled the pilot to take off. As the chopper rose, David turned in his seat to catch a final glimpse of the Sanctuary. It was ironic that a place designed to bring peace had brought him nothing but trouble.

Sam watched the chopper rise. Her vision was dimmed by hot, stinging tears. She slowed her steps, but not enough. An exposed root sent her sprawling.

Moments later, even as her breath came back in short gasps, Sam didn't move. Whether her loud sobbing came from the pain in her body or her heart, she couldn't be sure. She only knew she hurt with a hopelessness she had never known before. If only she had conquered her fears and talked to him last night. If only she had told him how she felt.

Sam didn't know how long she lay there. But when her breathing slowed and her sobs quieted she could still hear the flutter of helicopter rotors. The crunch of gravel nearby told her someone was coming.

"Samantha!" David let his crutches clatter to the ground as he dropped down beside her. "Talk to me, honey. Are you okay?"

Her mind was playing tricks on her. Maybe she was hurt more than she thought. But when she felt a hand gently stroke her cheek and draw the hair from her face, Sam knew David's presence was more than an illusion. She groaned, rolled stiffly to the side, and managed to sit up.

An arm settled around her shoulders and she let herself lean into its strength. "David?" she sniffed.

"Shhh, don't try to talk. Where does it hurt?" He examined her head and pulled a handkerchief out of his pocket to dab at the bloody abrasion on her forehead.

"It doesn't matter. You were leaving and I had to stop you, but you left . . ."

"That's why you were out here? You wanted to stop me?" Sam nodded. "I needed to tell you . . ."

"Save it." His voice was rough with emotion. "I already know how it is with you and Kansas." He reached for his crutches and added, "If you think you'll be okay for a few minutes, I'll go get someone to take you back to the house."

"No!" Samantha pulled at his arm. "Don't go. Please. I have to tell you . . . I did not come out here in my bathrobe to talk about Kansas. I came out to tell you I love you."

David leaned forward to rest his head against his bent knee. "You have a funny way of showing it," he said quietly. "What about Kansas?"

"I don't understand what you mean." Samantha heaved an exasperated sigh. "What does Kansas have to do with anything?"

David raised his head and looked at her. "Are you telling me you're not in love with Kansas?"

"In love? Of course not. Oh, I do love him, but as a friend." Sam turned from his accusing gaze and concentrated on picking small particles of gravel from the raw patches on her knees. She wanted to cry. Her head hurt; so did her knees and her arms.

"How could you think I'd be interested in Kansas? I'm married to you. And while we're on the subject, what about Jill? At first I thought maybe you and she . . . then I noticed how she looked at Kansas and I knew. But it wouldn't have mattered if she had wanted you. I would have fought to get you back. We can't give up, David." Sam paused to wipe her cheeks with the sleeve of her robe. "I love you so much."

David reached for her and framed her face with his hands. He followed the trail of her tears with tender kisses until he reached her trembling lips.

Going Home Together

It looks as though David and Samantha will be going home together after all. There are a lot of difficulties to be worked out, and if their relationship is like most of the others I've seen, their problems will continue to some degree or other. We'll check back with David and Samantha a little later, but now we'd better finish our packing and get ourselves back on board the *Kristiana* for the sail home.

It's time to go now. I climb aboard the yacht with mixed feelings, happy to be ending the journey yet wanting to linger. It's the same feeling I get whenever I read an inspirational book or attend an uplifting retreat; I'm always a little disappointed when it ends. The end means I have to come back into the real world. I have to go back to my husband, my home, and my life.

Heading for home means a lot of different things for different people, and as I watch the others come back to the ship I think about their journeys home.

Sam and David are going home together. Kansas and Jill? That's a bit more complicated. Jill will be going home to her small child, her work, the life she's made for herself as a single parent. As much as she would like to reconcile her relationship to Kansas, there are obstacles to overcome, broken pieces yet to be assembled. Kansas is returning home via the *Kristiana*. He and Jill will need to establish their relationship all over again. Both are willing to work at it. Both are hopeful that reconciliation can be accomplished. I wish I could give them a happy ending right now, but some things just take time.

Going Home Alone

Some of you, like my friend Abby, will be going home alone.

Abby told me one day over coffee that her husband was divorcing her. She was devastated. Divorce was against all she stood for as a Christian. She didn't want it, but she had little choice.

"We can talk all we want about having our needs met," Abby says now, "but someday we all have to wake up and face the hard fact that sometimes it just doesn't happen. I have no one to meet my sexual needs, my desire for security and protection. I work a nine-to-five job to make ends meet. As for sex, I try not to think much about it. When I want companionship, I have dear friends who care for me, support me in prayer, and listen to my problems."

Wounded and bleeding, a victim of brutal human conflict,

Abby is going home alone. Reconciliation for her is a matter of knowing that no matter what happens, God is with her. Abby will survive because her Source of life is not money, friends, her ex-husband, or her work, but God. Going home for Abby means continuing her struggle and continuing to learn about God's grace, mercy, forgiveness, and love. (Isn't that the struggle for all of us—married or not?)

Linda is going home alone as well. Her husband, Rob, died a few months ago. Many of her needs, too, go unmet. But she, like Abby, finds comfort in God. She keeps busy, works, and cares for her children. "I know that God will take care of my needs. That's not to say I don't get lonely. Sometimes I lie in bed at night and feel as if there's a big empty hole waiting to swallow me up. Sometimes panic hits me like a tidal wave and I think, *Oh, God, how am I ever going to make it without Rob?* Then somehow I do make it. People have told me, 'You seem so strong . . . how do you manage it?' 'It's the Lord,' I say, 'He carries me.' "

Carmen, as usual, is going home alone. She's single, and even though she didn't find her perfect mate on this cruise, she's feeling better about her singleness. She's no longer determined to find a man to make her complete—"I've found my identity—my completeness—in the Lord."

But whether we go home alone or together, we all have something in common. None of us will be going home to a place where all of our needs are met. Even when a man and woman work hard to meet each other's needs, our basic human imperfections won't allow any of us to be the perfect mate!

Take Reality With You!

Everyone has boarded the *Kristiana* now, and we've hoisted anchor. We wave good-bye to Reconciliation Bay. And as the moments slide by, the bay and all it represents fades into the horizon, leaving only a memory. David has relinquished his captain's duties to Kansas, whose mind seems to have drifted to some distant place.

"How is everything going, Kansas?" I ask. "You look worried."

"If you want to know the truth, I'm scared."

"Oh? You want to tell me about it?"

"I'm afraid it won't work . . . I mean, what if Jill is disappointed in me? What if I don't measure up?"

"In other words, you're asking me what will happen if you can't meet all her needs? You're worried that you won't be perfect for her?"

Kansas frowns. "I'd like to be, but . . ."

"Oh, Kansas," I sigh. "Have we gone through this entire book—taken this cruise—for nothing? Are you so mesmerized by Jill that you've forgotten all we've said about unrealistic expectations?"

"Guilty as charged, I guess. If anyone should remember the reality of imperfections in people, I should." Kansas grins as he throws his arm around my shoulder and hugs me. "Thanks, Mom, I needed that."

The fact is that we, like Kansas, may need to be reminded of reality over and over again. Actually, Kansas just reminded me of the reality that I'm almost old enough to be his mother. Fantasy would have me believing that I'll never age. Reality forces me to see the truth.

Only in dimly lit fairy tales does the glass slipper slip neatly onto the foot of Prince Charming's perfect woman. Reality crushes the glass slipper and splinters the false image of perfection. But reconciliation can mend the shattered pieces into something strong and sparkling.

Going Home to Imperfections

All of us are going home to a real world. I can be spiritual, kind, friendly, courteous, loving, and accepting—and still not have my hubby eating out of my hand. I can be as irresistible as a cocker spaniel, and it won't change the fact that my husband doesn't particularly want to hear about my latest diet or my frustration with flab. Let's face facts. We're going home to a real world where:

- A couple can have two Ph.D.s in communication and still have difficulty putting their feelings into words.
- Regardless of the length and quality of foreplay, women do not always enjoy sex. (Neither do men, for that matter.)
- He can bring her flowers, shower her with hugs and kisses, sing her love songs all day long, and she might still "have a headache" when they slip between the sheets at the end of the day.
- No matter how willing, sexy, and appealing a wife is, her husband is not always going to have an erection.
- No matter how much we give, no matter how much we sacrifice ourselves for our mates, no matter how much we love God, self, and others, we have no guarantee that our husbands or wives will return our love, will make the necessary changes for the relationship to survive, or will come to share our goals and desires.
- No matter how attractive a wife makes herself, she has no guarantee that Charlie won't decide to take off for Bermuda with his mistress.
- No matter what the beer commercials say, we can never really "have it all."

A number of years ago, singer Peggy Lee made popular a song called "Is That All There Is?" Many of us come to a place in our lives when we ask the same question. If I were to give an answer, I'd say, "Probably."

But I'm not trying to depress you with all this. I don't mean to suggest that relationships are always going to be miserable—not at all! Life is a confusing but exhilarating mixture of sorrow and joy, pain and promises. It's just that when we go home with illusions of "Rainbows and Lollipops"—a "Somewhere Out

There," "The Sun Will Come Out Tomorrow," and "The Grass Is Greener in the Next Pasture" perspective—we'll only end up disappointed. Isn't it better to face the reality that:

- Somewhere out there is a life woven with threads of laughter, joy, and freedom, as well as pain, tears, and disappointments;
- The sun *will* come out tomorrow, along with a rainbow, but sometime soon it's going to rain again; and
- The grass may be greener in other pastures, *but* it probably took a lot of manure and hard work to make it that way.

Being hurt, rejected, and disappointed in love and in life is a given. The quality of our lives depends greatly on how we choose to deal with it. Here are several choices:

- We can become bitter, gloomy, pessimistic, and drown in the sea of our despair.
- We can go on pretending we're in control, that we've got it all together. We can pretend our mate completely satisfies all our needs when he or she doesn't. We can keep up appearances within the bondage of the shell-like false selves we feel we must wear to survive.
- Or we can give up pretending and throw ourselves into finding joy in the life we have. We can choose to understand our human failings, frailties, and vulnerabilities. And we can rejoice in the knowledge that God loves us. As the Bible succinctly says, "You shall know the truth, and the truth shall make you free" (John 8:32).

The truth is that we are all fraught with human feelings. But the truth also is that once we recognize our need for a Savior, we cross the threshold into a world full of hope. We are not going home to a place where all our needs will be met, but we can go home content.

Going Home Content

Contentment is an inner peace that comes when we stop pretending that life could be wonderful "if only." In his letter to the Philippians, the apostle Paul writes, ". . . I have learned to be content in whatever circumstances I am" (4:11). What impresses me about this statement is that Paul didn't write it from a position of wealth and honor. He wrote from a prison cell. Paul had been whipped, rejected, vehemently opposed, and ridiculed. If Paul could find contentment in that position, then certainly I can find it in my life! What men and women need in one another is to find contentment regardless of their situations.

Paul goes on to say, "I know how to get along with humble means, and I also know how to live in prosperity; in any and every circumstance I have learned the secret of being filled and going hungry, both of having abundance and suffering need." The secret? "I can do all things through Him who strengthens me" (vv. 12–13).

Going home content means knowing God will protect us regardless of our circumstances. This contentment comes as we read our Bibles, study, pray, meditate, and become part of the community of believers. The secret is to focus on God and His strength, His ability, rather than on our own problems, failures, and inabilities.

Maybe you're asking, as Andrew did, "Are you saying that I should go home and be content even if my marriage is falling apart?"

Or perhaps, like Jennifer, you're saying, "Am I supposed to go on letting Frank abuse me?"

Going home content doesn't mean going home apathetic and brainless. To be content in God's strength is to walk forward with the power to right wrongs.

If you're going home to an abusive, manipulating spouse, God will grant you the courage and wisdom to stop the injustice. As I mentioned earlier, Jesus' style was to confront wrong, not placidly accept it. The pain He allowed others to inflict on Him was for a reason—to save us. It was His purpose to suffer and die for us so that He could be raised from the dead to give us the hope of eternal life. And though He warned us that suffering would be part of following Him, He never said we should invite suffering just for suffering's sake.

Going Home With a Good Foundation

The goal of this book has not been to teach you how to meet your partner's every need, nor has it been to teach you how to get someone to meet all your needs. Rather, I have hoped to reach deep into the inner recesses of what happens between men and women and locate the nerve centers, the places in the heart that dictate who we are and how we act toward others.

We can read a dozen books about how to meet his needs, her needs, your needs, and my needs. We can practice all the principles. And they are often very good principles. We can all benefit from learning about communicating with one another, avoiding conflict, and fighting fair. And if we are married, we will do well to learn the dynamics of sex and discover how we can better please our mates and enjoy sexual pleasures as God intended.

But a new paint job, new shutters, and a new roof won't keep a home intact if its foundation is rotting and crumbling.

What men and women most need in one another is a willingness to be remodeled from the bottom up—the inside out. We as individuals must start by establishing a firm foundation, concretely naming God as our most basic and necessary need.

As we continue to build on that foundation, we become reconciled to God, to ourselves, and to others; we become whole and able to move into the realm of reality. As we acknowledge our problems along the way, we also begin to find solutions to those problems.

... And Our Story Continues

Our fictional cruise ends with fond farewells and a hope that we can take another journey together sometime in the future. We all watch at the dock, brushing aside collective tears as Kansas waves good-bye and sails out of the harbor. And Samantha and David stand together on the dock with their arms around each other, united in the hope that they can somehow work things out.

Can they? Let's check in later and see.

We find Samantha and David reclining in lounge chairs in Samantha's beach house. Kansas, having visited the couple several times since their return home, joins them and lowers himself into an empty chair. "Mind if I join you?"

"Not at all," David says companionably. "Sam and I were just sitting here trying to decide where we want to live."

"Ah, yes," Kansas replies. "As I recall, that was a major problem between you two. Have you reached any conclusions?"

"Only one." Samantha swings her legs off the recliner and turnes to face Kansas and her husband. "Wherever we live, it will be together."

"We're going to stay here for another two months. I can't ride the range for a few weeks, anyway, and Samantha insists I need the salt air to recuperate, although I keep telling her the air in my part of Texas is a lot cleaner."

"Ahem . . . we'll stay in Texas for a couple of months," Sam says as she reaches for a glass of iced tea. "It's only fair that I give the ranch a trial. I was wrong to be so vehemently against living in a place I've never even visited."

"Wise thinking. But what about your business, Sam?" Kansas asks. "Custom Mates, Inc., needs you."

Sam gives David a shy smile before she answers. "I've decided that having a computer pick out your mate is a lot like the old-fashioned practice of having parents arrange marriages. I'm giving up the computer dating game. From now on, I plan to focus my attention on creating practical, educational software programs more suited to helping people make better choices in life."

Kansas grins that all-knowing grin that makes us wonder if he hadn't known the outcome of Samantha's computer mating system all along.

It appears that our charming couple have reconciled and gone home to a reality that isn't all that bad—at the moment, anyway. How about you? When all is said and done, I suppose we could say that what men and women need is to take an occasional vacation to Fantasy but, for the most part, live within the context of Reality and Reconciliation.

You may be wondering how I'm getting along in my real and reconciled world. Very well, actually. But I did have a momentary lapse the other day and was tempted to indulge in a bit of fantasy. My friend Lois and I went to the county fair. As we were wandering through the commercial booths, we happened upon a computer operator who boasted that she could tell us how ideally suited we were to our mates.

"I think I'll do this," I said. "It would make a cute ending for my book."

"Oh, okay; I'll wait if you want to," Lois said as she slowly went on ahead.

I hesitated a moment as I read more about the computer's claims. Suddenly I backed away. "I don't think I'll take a chance," I said. "After twenty-five years, I'd hate to find out I'd married the wrong man!"

Notes

Chapter 1   The Battle Rages On

1. Ann Landers, source unknown.
2. Shere Hite, *The New Hite Report, Women and Love: A Cultural Revolution in Progress* (New York: Knopf, 1987).
3. William Farrell, *Why Men Are the Way They Are* (New York: McGraw-Hill, 1986), 191–238.
4. Patricia H. Rushford, *What Kids Need Most in a Mom* (Old Tappan, New Jersey: Revell, 1986), 137–138.

Chapter 3   Adam's Island and The Secrets of a Man's Imagination

1. Annie Gottlieb, "What Men Need That Women Can't Give Them," *McCall's,* October 1983, 166.
2. Ibid.
3. Ibid.
4. Larry Crabb, *Inside Out* (Colorado Springs, Colorado: Navpress, 1988), 208–9.
5. Ibid., 211.
6. Joyce Brothers, *What Every Woman Should Know About Sex* (New York: Ballantine, 1981), 142.
7. Willard F. Harley, Jr., *His Needs, Her Needs* (Old Tappan, New Jersey: Revell, 1986), 41.

8. Daniel J. Levinson, *The Seasons of a Man's Life* (New York: Knopf, 1978), 57.
9. Ibid., 192–193.
10. Lois Leiderman Davitz, "My Ideal Woman," *McCall's*, July 1988, 148.

Chapter 4   Eve's Estuary: A Woman's World

1. Larry Crabb, *Inside Out* (Colorado Springs, Colorado: Navpress, 1988), 208–209.
2. James Dobson, *What Wives Wish Their Husbands Knew About Women* (Wheaton, Illinois: Tyndale, 1977).
3. Jann Mitchell, "Hite Readers Sound Off," *The Oregonian*, 29 October 1987, C5.
4. Jean Lush with Patricia H. Rusford, *Emotional Phases of a Woman's Life* (Old Tappan, New Jersey: Revell, 1987).

Chapter 5   Wishes, Falling Stars, and Dreams That Don't Come True

1. H. Norman Wright, *Marital Counseling: A Biblical, Behavioral, Cognitive Approach* (San Francisco, California: Harper & Row, 1983), 1.

Chapter 6   The Seven Dragons of Expectation Caves

1. Lucy Freeman, *What Do Women Want?* (New York: Human Sciences Press, 1978), 18.
2. Bruce Larson, *Faith for the Journey* (Old Tappan, New Jersey: Revell, 1982), 65.
3. H. Norman Wright, *Marital Counseling: A Biblical, Behavioral, Cognitive Approach* (San Francisco, California: Harper & Row, 1983), 1–2.
4. H. Norman Wright, *The Pillars of Marriage* (Glendale, California: Regal, 1979), 44.
5. Edith Schaeffer, *What Is a Family?* (Old Tappan, New Jersey: Revell, 1975), 74.

Chapter 7   How to Change the One You Love

1. James Dobson, *Love Must Be Tough*, (Waco, Texas: Word, 1983), 55. Format adapted.
2. Ibid., 65.

Chapter 8   Affairs, Lust, and Other Elements of Marital Decay

1. *Webster's New World Dictionary of the American Language* (New York: Warner, 1982), 359.

2. Richard J. Foster, *Money, Sex & Power* (San Francisco, California: Harper & Row, 1985), 13.
3. Ibid., 99.
4. Ibid., 121.
5. Ibid., 121–122.
6. Lewis B. Smedes, *Sex for Christians* (Grand Rapids, Michigan: Eerdmans, 1976), 210.
7. Randy C. Alcorn, *Christians in the Wake of the Sexual Revolution* (Portland, Oregon: Multnomah, 1985), 31.
8. Ibid., 201.
9. Dale Hanson Bourke, "Lois Mowday: Naive No Longer," *Today's Christian Woman*, May/June 1989, 42.
10. Judith Viorst, *Love & Guilt & the Meaning of Life, Etc.* (New York: Simon & Schuster, 1979), 3.

Chapter 9   The Trouble With Divorce

1. Charles R. Swindoll, *Strike the Original Match: Rekindling and Preserving Your Marriage Fire* (Portland, Oregon: Multnomah, 1980), 136.
2. David Neff, "The Painless-Divorce Myth," *Christianity Today*, 12 May 1989, 17.
3. Dale Evans Rogers, *Woman: Be All You Can Be* (Old Tappan, New Jersey: Revell, 1980), 97.
4. Judith Wallerstein and Joan Kelley, *Surviving the Breakup* (New York: Basic Books, 1980).
5. Neff, "Painless-Divorce Myth," 17.
6. Diane Medved, "A Case Against Divorce," *Reader's Digest*, May 1989, 97.

Chapter 10   Secrets of the Past

1. John Bradshaw, *Bradshaw On: The Family* (Deerfield Beach, Florida: Health Communications, 1988), 66.
2. William Kirwan, *Biblical Concepts for Christian Counseling: The Case for Integrating Psychology and Theology* Grand Rapids, Michigan: Baker, 1984), 81–82.
3. Bradshaw, *Bradshaw On: The Family*, 20.

Chapter 11   Reconciling With God

1. Archimandrite Sophrany, *His Life Is Mine*, tr. Rosemary Edmonds (Crestwood, New York: St. Vladimir's Seminary Press, 1977), 12–13.
2. Ibid., 13.

Chapter 12   Reconciling to Self

1. Marc Feigen Fasteau, *The Male Machine* (New York: McGraw-Hill, 1974), 1–2. Format adapted.

2. Ibid.
3. Jay Adams, *The Biblical View of Self-Esteem, Self-Love, and Self-Image* (Eugene, Oregon: Harvest House, 1986), 79, 106.
4. Alexander Lowen, *Narcissism: Denial of the True Self* (New York: Collier/Macmillan, 1985), ix.
5. Ibid.
6. Ibid.
7. John Bradshaw, *Healing the Shame That Binds You* (Deerfield Beach, Florida: Health Communications, 1988), viii–ix.
8. Patricia H. Rushford, "Become Like a Child Again," in *What Kids Need Most in a Mom* (Old Tappan, New Jersey: Revell, 1986), 104.
9. John Bradshaw, *Bradshaw On: The Family* (Deerfield Beach, Florida: Health Communications, 1988), 64.
10. M. Scott Peck, *The Different Drum: Community Making and Peace* (New York: Simon & Schuster, 1987), 54–55.

Chapter 13 Reconciling With One Another

1. Oswald Chambers, *My Utmost for His Highest* (Westwood, New Jersey: Barbour, 1935), 217.
2. M. Scott Peck, *The Different Drum: Community Making and Peace* (New York: Simon & Schuster, 1987), 58.
3. Phyllis Schlafly, *The Power of the Christian Woman* (Cincinnati, Ohio: Standard, 1981), 10.
4. Don Williams, *The Apostle Paul and Women in the Church* (Ventura, California: Regal, 1977).
5. Rick Bella, "It's Never Matri-moany," *The Oregonian*, 23 June 1989, D3.
6. M. Scott Peck, *The Road Less Traveled* (New York: Simon & Schuster, 1978), 127–128.
7. Phyllis Diller, *Phyllis Diller's Marriage Manual* (Greenwich, Connecticut, Fawcett, 1967), 15.
8. Ouida, in Phyllis Hobe, ed., *Tapestries of Life* (Carmel, New York: Guideposts, 1974), 120.